CRISIS
PASTORAL CARE

CRISIS
PASTORAL CARE

A Police Chaplain's Perspective

Thomas W. Shane, D. Div.

HOHM PRESS
Prescott, Arizona

Cover Design: Accurance, Bloomington, Illinois

Interior Design and Layout: Kadak Graphics, Prescott, Arizona. www.kadakgraphics.com

Library of Congress Cataloging-in-Publication Data

Shane, Thomas W.
Crisis pastoral care : a police chaplain's perspective / Thomas W. Shane.
    p. cm.
Includes index.
ISBN 978-1-935387-22-0 (trade paper : alk. paper)
1. Chaplains, Police. 2. Crisis intervention (Mental health services) I. Title.
BV4375.5.S43 2011
253.088'3632--dc23
                        2011025740

HOHM PRESS
P.O. Box 2501
Prescott, AZ 86302
800-381-2700
www.hohmpress.com

This book was printed in the U.S.A. on recycled, acid-free paper using soy ink.

To my wife Linda and our children
Kimberly, Mark, Michael, and Sara

CONTENTS

INTRODUCTION

For three decades a large part of my ministry has been as a police chaplain. And although the work I got paid for was as a hospital chaplain and as a certified supervisor with the Association for Clinical Pastoral Education, my time as a police chaplain was a large part of my life and just as dear to my heart. Most parish clergy will likely experience many aspects of the crisis work I describe in this book, and I hope to tell the story in a way that enlightens this often hidden and inevitably sad world of work with cops.

Other authors and other resources will do the important job of outlining the theory and practice of crisis intervention. My intent is to tell stories, so that those who are called to do intervention will have a sense of what the reality is like. Theological education can get lost in a world of ideas. When this happens, theology is at risk of being dehumanized rather than grounded in the human condition. Sin is not a concept. It is the experience of Jack who thought his wife was having an affair, and so took his revolver from the car's glove box, walked into the living room where she was watching a movie with their children, and shot her to death.

I am writing to describe the world of police chaplaincy. Many times when law enforcement personnel are needed, chaplains should have a presence as well. Local clergy are likewise involved, if not initially, then with the long term care of those who are affected by tragedy. In this book I describe a number of circumstances where those in law enforcement encounter people in great distress (legally, socially, psychologically, interpersonally, medically and spiritually). I then offer representative case stories where clergy are involved in providing pastoral care.

All the incidents are true accounts of my work as a police chaplain, and in each case particular faith matters are dramatically revealed. Understandably some details have been altered to protect the privacy of those involved, yet each story is grounded in an authentic event.

CLINICAL PASTORAL CARE

Clinical pastoral care is significantly different from academic pastoral care because it is grounded in the nitty-gritty of the human experience. This book presupposes that this pastoral care includes three parts: a **personal arena**, a **skill arena**, and a **conceptual arena**; and that all three always unfold at once and must be managed.

Each chaplain needs to be constantly aware of what is happening to him or her personally in the pastoral experience. This includes everything that is going on in the chaplain's life which he or she brings to the moment and which may have a bearing on the work if it is not adequately managed. Such pre-existing experiences might include health concerns, marriage issues, or even joyous personal matters like the birth of a child. Any of these events might impact one's ability to be present with someone. Besides the state of mind a chaplain brings to the pastoral event from his or her personal life, the event itself often calls forth issues which impact how a chaplain gives care. Seeing a significantly injured child who is similar in age to one a chaplain knows and loves may impede effective care.

The skill arena has to do with the chaplain's need to decide what intervention is appropriate in a given event. There are many pastoral-intervention possibilities, and the chaplain must make an assessment to discern what will be the most effective way to provide care.

The theoretical arena covers a chaplain's beliefs—the many ways he or she might conceptualize or understand what is going on. Such beliefs are drawn from theology, psychology, ethics, family systems, and grief work principles.

By its very nature, ministry as a profession is more general than it is specialized, and as a rule it is centered in parish life, as it should be. Some clergy extend their interests to unique settings such as hospitals, prisons, universities, or the military. Many of us in specialized settings believe it is imperative for the church to go into the world to share the Good News and not just invite everyone to come to church. Some are in crisis—too wounded, too filled with shame, or confused about how to access the church—so we go to them.

SOMEONE ELSE'S WORLD

Only when a chaplain knows who he or she *is*, both personally and professionally, can they move with ease and integrity among other professionals with different roles. I am a clergy, not a cop; a pastor, not a therapist, and a preacher, not a physician. The reality is that clergy in specialized settings are working in someone else's world and have to play by their rules. A lot of things occur which may seem strange to us or even hostile to our beliefs and training.

Our task is to learn to suspend judgment so that we have the opportunity of creating a pastoral alliance from which we can appropriately pick and choose the times to care and the times to confront. One cannot overlay a church world and its protocol onto a homicide scene and expect the language, procedures, and style to be the same.

The vignettes which follow reflect my belief in the power of story and demonstrate my own grappling with the difficulties in entering someone else's world. Over the years I have been part of a great many painful human experiences. I have witnessed the terrible results of broken promises, heard the piercing cries of anguish, known the bitter taste of despair. What I hope to share is the reality of the tears, not the theory of grief.

Much of what I say about emergency ministry grows out of my work as a chaplain to the law enforcement agencies in Harvey County, Kansas. I trust that these stories will deepen your understanding of what might genuinely serve another if or when fate calls you to stand in the presence of human crisis.

WORKING WITH COPS

Law enforcement is a tight fraternity, and it is very difficult to gain acceptance within a profession that puts one in potential contact with sorrow, where one must make immediate and often life threatening decisions, and where there is danger at every turn. Even though the job is generally routine, it can explode into chaos in the briefest moment. Cops want to know they can depend on their partner. They want to know they can say "bullshit" and not have some preacher scold them for their language. And if you've ever been around cops you'll know they can be, at times, both crude and offensive. One can wish that the language were sweeter and more compassionate. But don't rush to judgment. Listen closely to the underlying message. The rough words are just tough ways to keep the world of sorrow at a distance. One can't come in close contact with such agony and not be impacted by it. The chaplain who listens to the deeper truth and is not put off by the presented language will likely be more successful. And, when a chaplain sees the same atrocity and feels the same repulsion at pieces of brain on the wall or slivers of skull on the floor, then he or she is more likely able to build credibility with the team.

A great deal of time and the willingness to accept the risks of a cop's world earns a chaplain his place. I had to learn to be there as a clergy first, before I could value a cop's role and task. On too many occasions I was seduced into seeing myself as law enforcement instead of chaplain. After all, I carried a badge, I was commissioned as a reserve officer, and I was assigned radio number 606. But time and again the officers would call me back to my primary identity by the way they addressed me. "Hi, Rev. Glad you're here." It mattered to them that I was "The Rev."

One has to be willing to see life from a cop's perspective. Perspectives are interesting. They are not right or wrong, only points of view. Still, they have a claim on the human experience, and if a police chaplain is to serve effectively, he or she had better understand a cop's viewpoint.

Clergy generally lift up hope and possibility for peace and reconciliation. That's a worthy goal. Cops, on the other hand, are more street-wise and are less idealistic. If preachers pray for peace, it is cops who are called to stop the conflict in the living rooms where family disturbances have turned from disagreement to chaos, and family blood is spilled on the carpet. Make no mistake about it, life on the streets is rough and raw. Naïve preachers are, quite frankly, in the way.

Take your time, and develop a trust level with officers.
Find some way to authentically enter the world
of law enforcement.
Establish trust with administration.
Maintain confidentiality.
Be available, crises happen at any time.
Learn the language and procedures of law enforcement.
Learn the art of Pastoral Presence and realize
that not all things can be fixed.
Crisis work is chaotic and upsetting.

THE REAL MOMENT

The flashing red lights bounced off the darkened windows of the homes along Main Street, as I went Code 3 with the officer to the scene. I sat quietly and felt my stomach tighten into knots, listened to the grim talk from the radio. But there was also a sense of excitement, or maybe anticipation, as we hurried along. Our small town streets were nearly deserted at 2 AM, but to watch what few cars there were pull aside and give us passage seemed to make the point that something important had happened. Shootings and attempted murder are never routine. They stand as reminders of how sinful and flawed humankind is. Until I became a police chaplain, such moments were merely the plots of television programs or mystery writers. Now they were a part of my work.

What a strange mixture of interests and jobs: the ministry and law enforcement. It wasn't something I ever had fantasies about. Law enforcement was a world apart from me. Not until I grudgingly accepted an assignment as a jail chaplain during my clinical education did I discover the drama and fascination of law enforcement work. Not until I looked deeply and intentionally into the hopeless eyes of victims scarred by crime and desperation, not until I heard the wailing of parents who were told that a cherished child was fatally injured in an auto accident, not until I felt how such moments put one in touch with the raw nerve ends of human suffering could I sense that as a chaplain I might have a chance—perhaps even a responsibility—to bring a word of healing and hope to those in critical need. At such times the church is often not present, and yet I learned how indispensable such a ministry is. Not until I saw an officer put his arm around a grieving child who stood shaking in grief because a parent was just killed did I *know* what I so hoped was true: that cops care. They too tremble in fear when working a disaster and yet stand firm and resolute, ignoring their own inner feelings because another needs the help they can give. That's what courage is: doing what must be done, however repulsive and difficult it is, because another needs help.

Fred, the officer I was riding with, continued to tell me the details as they were known. An angry man supposed that his girlfriend had another lover and could not tolerate such a thought. With no apparent effort to work things out, or even to confirm his suspicions, and with only the force of his blinding rage to give him direction, he got his .45 and went to her home, intending to kill her as she slept. With all reason giving way to blind fury, he kicked open the front door and stalked her as if she were a sportsman's prey. With her two children screaming in helpless hysteria, he shot her and then left, as if his day's work was through. Though badly injured, the woman and her terrified children went next door for help. The neighbors called 911.

We turned the corner into a maze of flashing red lights. "We think he was alone," Fred continued, "but there is some possibility that someone else was here too. We've got the suspect downtown, but we're still searching the area just in case."

Just in case! Still, my palms were not sticky so much from fear of another night time stalker as from anxiety about what I might have to see. I don't cozy up to human carnage very well. I don't enjoy seeing another human being broken and torn. And yet that's part of police chaplaincy.

Just as we shut down the siren and red lights of the squad car, the ambulance doors slammed shut and carried off the victim to the local hospital. I felt relief knowing that I wouldn't have to see the woman suffering. Inside the neighbor's house were grim reminders of the ugly moment. Several officers walked about carrying out a variety of tasks. There were bright red splotches on the white carpet, bearing silent testimony to the evil moment just past. Kneeling over them, the terrified neighbor trembled as she tried to wash the stains clean. She had been sleeping normally just a short while ago when she was awakened by desperate screaming and relentless pounding at her back door. Now she talked nervously to herself and tried to coax the blood from her new shag carpet. But it would not leave. The fresh blood had stained it as thoroughly as it had the lives of all involved.

And then I saw them. My heart ached at the scene I noticed in the corner of the living room. On the couch, stiffly and silently, sat the two children of the critically injured woman. They neither smiled nor cried—as if they hoped they might slip through this chaos unnoticed and therefore untouched. In the rush of things, the children seemed almost forgotten. With only strangers to care for them, their wide-eyed looks marked them as adrift in a raging sea of terror. I sat down beside them and hoped I might offer some comfort.

"What if he comes back to shoot us, too?" In a shallow, whispered voice the little boy looked at me. Even the presence of a room full of armed officers was not enough to calm him. After all, he and his sister had heard the roar of the gun as it exploded and shattered their mother, and also their lives. It was real to them. If such terror could happen once, why couldn't it happen again? The girl sat unmoving on the couch, but her eyes glistened with tears of anger and sadness. Her brother put his arms around her, as if to promise he would try to make it right. I too tried to reassure them of their safety, at least in that moment.

Soon enough, all the professionals on the crime scene went on to other tasks. Some went back to the hospital to gather information. Some went next door where the shooting took place to look for evidence, and some went into the still, dark night to make sure there was, indeed, no one else lurking in the backyard or alley. Perhaps the look of anxious determination on the officers' faces told the story best of all.

Cops sometimes overreact and sometimes they talk too rough. But on this night, they showed compassion to two scared kids. As they continued their investigation I was left alone with the two youngsters and a numbed neighbor. I listened again and again to their story and, in so doing, came face to face with evil and fear and destruction in their trembling and ashen-eyed faces.

I

RELATIONSHIPS

Pastoral care is never just a task to do or a procedure to follow. It always occurs within the context of a relationship. It is just as true for chaplains working with cops as it is for parish clergy working with parishioners. Sometimes the relationships are professional in nature—a chaplain providing pastoral care to an officer, or to the victim of a crime or an accident. Sometimes the relationships are personal, and the chaplain will worry about the safety of an officer doing a dangerous task. But there are always relationships, and that is good.

Sometimes it is hard to account for friendships. Perhaps the magic of common interests draws friends together. Then again, maybe it is our differences that offer intrigue and curiosity and which, in their own way, are the necessary sparks for a friendship to develop. Respect surely plays a part too. Often as not, in a viable friendship people find aspects of the other's life, personality, or work that they value and respect, and a personal alliance is nourished. Sometimes you just like someone and can't say why.

Whatever it is, if it all works out just so, friendships are born. And if things never develop far enough for you call it a friendship, there is always a concern for the officers you work with. In a real sense, a chaplain's law enforcement community becomes his or her parish.

Once you have gained a trusted place in the department, officers will turn to you for assistance. Sometimes they ask you to perform their weddings. Sometimes they stop by because a child is ill or in trouble.

The glamour and romance of a cop's life comes mostly from the movies. A cop's life is a tough life. By its very nature, the work involves regular contact with those in the culture who are troubled or who cause trouble. To cops, such troublemakers are often known as "scuzballs" or "dirtbags." Cops are called names as well, and are often the target of verbal abuse, spitting, hitting, kicking, biting, and at times, knifings and shootings. Drunks may throw up all over the insides of the squad car and cops have to clean up the vomit. People get scared in situations of emergency; sometimes they lose control of bowel or bladder function. Only if you've truly entered a cop's world can you authentically understand the way idealism drifts toward cynicism and why that happens. I have little doubt that cops by and large enter the profession because it is one way to help people. Cops seem to hang on to that vision even when the reality of the work threatens their early idealism. Along with the possibility of helping others, however, there is the continual frustration and cynicism born of their day-to-day grind. I guess cops get used to the teenage street-corner kids who flip them off and yell, "Hey, motherfucker pig. Kiss my ass!" as the police car drives by. Not a major event, certainly, and most cops can even discount it easily enough. Still, they hear it. They know it reflects a community attitude that is anti-authority, even when the authority primarily seeks to work for the community's welfare.

You can't spend years riding shotgun with officers without realizing that you have become friends with many of them. You can't work a grisly homicide scene and not discover the human side of a cop. During those long hours of working together you inevitably share stories of your life with one another, and that sharing fosters the growth of a friendship.

MAX

I was surprised when Max said I could ride with him for part of his shift. It had taken courage for me to even ask him. Max seemed so aloof and unapproachable that I wasn't sure he would accept me as a partner. He was tough; not mean, just reserved, quiet, and strong. A veteran with street smarts, Max was the one deputy you hoped would back you if something really bad happened. His crewcut and his square jaw sometimes reminded me of a college fraternity brother, a drill instructor in the Marine Corps. Max looked this part with his steely eyes, and like a drill sergeant he commanded with an edge to his voice.

When I got together with Max I had only been a law enforcement chaplain for a few months and most of my ride-along time had been with the city police. Now I was in the county and things were different. Personal connections were not yet established. It generally takes a long time to break into any new community, but finding your place with cops is particularly tough.

After all, as the potential for life-threatening trouble is always one call away, cops need to feel confident that you won't get in the way and that you can take care of yourself. They also want to know that you'll be willing to look after their back, if it comes to that. Cops want to be themselves and not feel that the chaplain will judge them. Partnered with Max, I was clearly the rookie, and a volunteer one at that.

On that first shift together we rode in silence for a long time before he spoke. "It's OK for you to ride with me, but you need to know that some days I don't talk much. Don't take it personally. On other days, I'll open up. It's the way I am."

I did learn, and he was right about his style. Over the years I would spend many Saturday nights with Max, much of it in silence. I'll never really understand how it happened, but from that day on, we became friends—good friends. Max was the kind you could turn to when your world fell apart. Years later, I needed that friendship and that silence when I faced breakdowns along my own road. In those times I was glad for our rides in silence. Max always understood.

One evening a typically cryptic phone message told me news that was hard to hear. "This is Max. Thought I'd let you know I turned in my retirement papers today. I've got three weeks of vacation, and then I'm done." A typical Max response—short and to the point. I was shocked. Max and I are the same age. How could he retire ahead of me? How could his career pass by so quickly? After thirty years of law enforcement—ten years with the city, twenty with the county—was it really time to call it quits? One day it seems you have a whole career ahead of you; the next day it's all over.

But even a quiet guy like Max doesn't silently fade into the night. The guys who worked with him for thirty years wouldn't allow that. There were too many stories to tell, memories to honor, debts to pay. His buddies insisted on a celebration and a roast, and so a couple hundred of us gathered at the local Elks Club to say thanks and good luck.

Good spirit was all around us that night, yet still I was sad. For twenty of Max's thirty years on the job here, I had ridden with him on most Saturday nights. I was going to miss him. My feelings were understandable, and so were his. When it was Max's turn to speak, he told us that he'd only been emotional twice in his life—once when his dad died, and tonight. "This is harder than I thought it would be," he said. Somehow we all knew that.

As I listened to his friends roast him, a host of my own memories rushed in. Once, during the Kansas State Fair, we drove west on US 50 as mile after mile of east-bound traffic hummed by and seemed to lull us to sleep. A long way off, but coming straight toward us, I noticed a tiny Ford Pinto that had tried to pass but couldn't find a way back into the fair traffic. Somehow stuck in our lane, it was hurtling at us like a missile, and our fate seemed doomed.

Was Max oblivious to the danger? Was he in some kind of hypnotic trance? I began to sweat, but still refused to be a "back-seat-driver."

Surely Max saw this impending tragedy, I figured. But still he continued on in his typically unperturbed silence—either very brave or sound asleep, I thought to myself.

Finally, with only moments to spare, I screamed out in dread, "Max! We're going to crash!"

In a last second maneuver, he drove his black Jimmy into the ditch, narrowly missing the little Pinto. That woke us up! It woke up the whole county, too, as Max quickly radioed dispatch, "902 Newton, we just got run off the road by some damn car. It won't stop and we're 10-32!" The chase was on!

When we eventually stopped the errant driver, we discovered a terrified and inexperienced teenage girl, not the fleeing felon we had expected. Reliving that moment years later, we could both laugh a bit; but at the time, it raised the hair on the back of my neck. For Max too.

I also recalled a day when the March skies turned into a boiling mass of seething clouds that twisted themselves into vicious tornados and ripped the tiny town of Andover, Kansas, to shreds. Max and I went to Andover with a host of other deputies and spent the evening walking the darkened streets, stepping over the broken dreams of the townspeople, amid destroyed homes and shattered cars looking for bodies in the trees and survivors in the rubble.

And I will always remember the summer evening when, as I worked in my front yard, Max drove up, stood stoically by his black and white Jimmy with his steely eyes fixed on me and announced that he had requested a transfer to third shift. "Why?" I asked.

"Because I'm tired of pulling children out of the grill work of drunk drivers!" he remarked. "I was first on the scene at the fatality last week. I pulled the two girls out of the grill work and I took the pictures. It's enough for a while." Even the toughest deputies have tender hearts when children are killed.

Underneath the expressionless face that Max typically wore was the compassion I always knew was there. It never took much effort for me to see beneath his gruff exterior to discover how caring he was. Only the public and those who broke the law were fooled by Max's hard exterior.

During months of my own hard times, when my dad's illness steadily worsened and I sat at his bedside watching him steadily shrink in vitality, Max took the course I taught on death and dying at the community college. Attentive in class and insightful in his own way, he listened to what I tried to teach about the nature of grief and suffering, and where and how hope is found. And when my dad's life came to a merciful end, Max was supportive with a simple card and gift of flowers. His kindness warmed my sad heart.

And not so long after that, the world of sorrow shifted in his direction as Max faced his own crisis when his dad followed a similar journey to death. Like me, Max watched his father fail steadily day by day until there was no more health and vitality left to fight. The old man gave in at last to the ultimate and inevitable destiny that will one day claim us all.

When you watch your father die and you can't do anything to stop the process, you realize how helpless you are. Even if you are tough and private by nature, the death of your parent touches your spirit. And yet, if you have a friend like Max who knows a type of "dark night of the soul" and how to be present, then the darkness is less terrifying and not so lonely. Max was there for me and I tried to be there for him.

After his friends had offered their own memories, it was Max's turn. One by one he thanked us in some personal way.

I was touched when he offered me "a special thanks," noting that I had taught him "that you can mix faith and law enforcement together; and it works." Then he reminded me about the time that my Dodge truck broke down in western Kansas as he and I returned after a fly fishing trip to Colorado, and how we nearly melted to death in the 109-degree heat. And we laughed.

In thirty years of law enforcement, any chaplain or police officer will have witnessed a lot of fights and plenty of Code-3 runs to fatality accidents. He or she will have been in car chases and worked homicides. If you live in Kansas, for instance, you will have spent every spring in some open prairie, looking intently at the tumbling green clouds to watch for that ominous rotation that breeds a tornado. You will remember the tiny towns blown to pieces by these compelling acts of nature.

But probably what you remember most of all are your colleagues: the deputies with whom you rode the back roads of the county year after year; those men or women who put aside every difference to stand by you when the chips were down. These memories you never forget.

I think there are no better friends than cops, and for me no better friend than Max. His retirement didn't end our friendship, of course; but it certainly changed the way we spent our time together. Change always requires us to let go of the past so we can reach for the future. Yet we do so with an edge of sadness.

I will miss my Saturday nights with Max.

CHIP'S STORY

I looked down from the chancel to the sanctuary at the large gathering of mourners who had come to say goodbye to Paula. The church was filled to capacity. Even the aisles were full. So were most of the classrooms in the education building where the service was being sent by audio so that the overflow crowd could listen. It was an impressive show of support for Paula's husband Chip, a state trooper, and his two sons.

The large turnout of friends wasn't unexpected; it was a way to share the grief of a beloved colleague whose wife who died an untimely death.

Earlier, before I entered the sanctuary, a friend of mine, a retired cop, had pulled me aside and whispered, "I'll be praying for you. This will be a tough funeral to do. I know you are close to Chip and his family. This one's personal for you." His acknowledgement touched my heart. It *was* a difficult service to do.

Chip and I had been friends for years. I was a reserve deputy and chaplain with the county sheriff's department and had worked professionally with him on a number of death notifications. Our professional work lead naturally to a new closeness. We learned to know each other, and well.

On the morning of his beloved wife's funeral, I swallowed the lump in my throat and vowed to offer Chip and everyone present the most caring and healing funeral service I could provide. Law enforcement personnel are often unwilling or unable to share their feelings of grief out of the mistaken belief that to do so is a sign of weakness. But in fact, it takes great courage.

Chip sat with his sons Andy and Jake on either side of him, as a friend of the family sang. The beautiful sound filled the sanctuary with tender feeling, and set the tone for the entire service.

I watched as Chip reached out to his sons and held their hands. Tears streamed down all their cheeks. From my perspective it was as good a union of courage and grief as anyone could hope for.

I was flooded with memories of my service with Chip. One Saturday night, as we launched into our usual conversation about our children, the State Patrol dispatch suddenly sent out an urgent message to all area troopers. "Attention all units. Report of shots fired. Trooper down on the turnpike at the Wellington rest area. Repeat, trooper down. All units respond."

In seconds, life transitioned from our personal conversation to an immediate awareness of life and death reality. When the risks were high, and the intensity level rose to this point, Chip was all business. A trooper was wounded!

With single-minded focus he raced our patrol car to the scene along I-135, passing other motorists as if they were parked. That was the Chip I knew.

On this morning of Paula's funeral I also remembered the times of joyful sharing, like those holiday banquets when my wife Linda and I would sit with Chip and Paula. Both our wives were quiet and thoughtful people who found in each other a kindred spirit.

And then one day we learned that Paula had been diagnosed with cancer. She began to receive treatment at the hospital where I worked. When she came in for chemotherapy I would meet Chip for coffee. Pastoral care often occurs *on the spot*, in public places like cafeterias, and over cups of coffee. And chaplains learn the art of hearing the deeper truth about unspoken fears and looming sorrow that is not yet named, but lurks just outside ordinary conversation.

I clearly remembered the day I saw Paula in her room at the hospital and she was able to tell me that, "If this doesn't work out, my greatest fear is leaving Chip alone." Life may end, but love never does. And Paula had an endless supply of love for her family.

It was a Saturday morning when the hospital chaplain called to tell me that Paula was back in, and that the prognosis was grim. I will always appreciate the chaplain's sensitivity—she knew that Paula and I were friends. Then, with words I will never forget, the chaplain said, "You need to hurry. This won't be long."

I found Chip and the boys standing at Paula's bedside. Their eyes were sad, their faces strained with grief. It's hard to watch someone you love slip slowly but relentlessly from life as we know it. At such moments, we humans are on holy ground. A touch on the shoulder, a hug, and a quiet presence conveys how much you care. The monitors next to Paula's bed showed only a weak heart pattern, barely enough to sustain life. And then the lines were flat. Our vigil was over.

So many memories from so many years—they all flashed through my mind during the service. When it was over, a state patrol honor guard of many cars escorted Paula's coffin out of the church and to the cemetery. A fitting tribute to a gracious and courageous woman.

When my wife and I moved to Houston a few years ago to be near family, Chip knew it was a bittersweet decision for me. I would miss my friends in the law enforcement and hospital communities. But real friendships don't die. They take on new forms and must be nurtured in fresh ways. The ones that are solid stand the test of time and distance.

II

PROMINENT PASTORAL THEMES

In seminary I took a course on theology, along with every other divinity student. I found the subject rather dry and academic. I could agree that theology was a necessary course, giving me an exposure to the critical thinking of the church's greatest thinkers over the last two thousand years. But it seemed an academic enterprise designed more for my head than my heart. Theology seemed removed from the ordinary world of the people I knew.

A couple of years later, I took a unit of clinical pastoral education at Presbyterian Medical Center in Denver, Colorado, and my whole mindset about theology changed. Suddenly all the issues I was exposed to in my theology class were vibrantly, passionately alive, because I experienced them not in textbooks, but in the context of the living human canvas of people who were in the midst of their own crises.

That shift in my attitude was personally enlightening, and it made clear that contextual theology is the basis for academic theology, and includes the heart as well as the head.

One afternoon I was summoned to the bedside of a young woman who had been hurt in an automobile accident. Her physical injuries were minimal, but the assault to her soul was significant. She and her female passenger were on their way to a wedding. A second vehicle failed to yield at a stop sign and crashed into the side of her car, killing her passenger. Both women were to have been bridesmaids.

"Tell me chaplain," cried the driver, "how could such a dreadful thing happen?" Questions of the perceived absence of God, the struggle with prayer, why bad things happen to good people, and how to forgive the errant driver were keenly evident. This was not a philosophical discussion, this was an exploration of theology growing from a human experience.

There are many such moments that confront chaplains who work in law enforcement. I have selected four themes—sin, forgiveness, the absence of God and prayer—that I met frequently in my ministry. Each of these theological issues is grounded in the human experience. Chaplains will routinely address these and many more in their crisis care.

SIN

People commit all manner of dreadful events against others, and it is important for clergy who work as police chaplains to understand the depth of sin they face while providing pastoral care.

After experiencing years of marital discord, a man took his children to a local lake for what they surely hoped would be a day of fun. But, with his heart filled with unresolved rage at his estranged wife, this father stabbed his children to death in an attempt to hurt her. Then, feeling some level of remorse, he stabbed himself before calling 911.

His wound was not life threatening, and he was admitted to a local hospital for emergency surgery. Knowing the story about the murder of his children, the staff was angry at him, wondering how a father could do such a thing to his own children.

As chaplains, the words of theology come easily to us: sin, redemption, forgiveness. They are "the stuff" of theology. "Christ died for your sins!" "Repent and be forgiven." They are church slogans we often accept without much thought. Certainly they hold a piece of truth, but we rarely reflect on them. They are the sacred counterparts to secular truisms like "honor your country." Who can argue with the basic value of any of these slogans? But their bland universalism is their undoing. Generic truth is empty truth. Universal truth is too easily ignored. It has no bite. A lot of theology seems to float around in the air above life. Meanwhile, human beings live on the earth. Theology should be as real as every human encounter a pastor has—born of tears and laughter, broken hearts and shame. Theology actually *begins* with the human experience, followed by a reflection on that experience.

Sin, for example, is a separation from God and is the bad we do and the good we do not do. But sin is usually held as a concept or an abstraction. As such, we can say we are opposed to it, but miss its destructive power to the human spirit. Sometimes, the abhorrent sense of sin hooks our own dark side and we crave a closer encounter with it, though usually from a safe, distant perspective. We observe it out of our curiosity. We preach against it, but only in an abstract sense. More often than not we keep a safe distance from sin and avoid a close personal encounter with it. But evil is as real as a 911 call from a frantic father, screaming for the dispatcher, "She's dead! My daughter's dead. Send help!"; and sin is the constant companion of every police chaplain. No generic abstraction, sin is cold and brutal, like homicide.

RITA

I sat in the back of the sheriff's car while he drove. Rita sat in front of me, her hands tightly clasped half in prayer, half in dread. She nervously bit at her lower lip. As we drove down First Street, Rita kept her head down, looking only at the stainless steel handcuffs that kept her wrists together. From time to time, the radio crackled routine radio traffic, a constant reminder that this was no ordinary car and this no ordinary trip.

Just at the edge of town and a hundred yards before the interstate we turned north into the cemetery. Rita seemed to pull deeper into herself as if to seek someplace to hide. As we drove slowly through the winding gravel road toward the open grave and the small gathering of family and friends, I watched as Rita began to tremble. And so did I. "Nine-o-one and 606 are 10-23 at the cemetery with our subject. Ending mileage is 63,234" spoke the sheriff to the communications center.

Before us was a simple wooden casket with a plain spray of flowers. An on-call pastor, tapped for funerals of families who have no regular church, stood at the head of the gravesite, ready to begin as soon as we arrived.

The sheriff opened Rita's door and helped her out of the tan Chrysler. With a soft word of comfort he spoke to her, "I know this is tough, Rita, but it's the right thing to do. It won't take long and we'll leave as soon as it's over. Don't worry. You'll be OK."

In silence, she nodded her head and acknowledged the wisdom of his words.

I was glad the sheriff was there. I was glad he was big. I was glad he had a radio. And I was glad he was armed. I looked about the small crowd and knew for the first time ever that I was in the presence of hatred, and though it was directed at Rita and not me, I could feel it too. A grieving, older woman named Helen, the mother of the dead man, sat at the head of the casket, her eyes downcast, her mouth clenched shut as tears slipped down her cheeks. Next to her sat her two grandchildren, the two young sons of Rita and the deceased. One boy was ten, the other eight. Each seemed lost in this world of chaos and despair.

Two brothers of the deceased stood behind their mother along with an odd assortment of cousins and friends; it was this group that scared me. If mom looked down in grief, if the two boys stared all glassy eyed into space, the men of the group glared at Rita, the sheriff, and me in bitter, defiant rage.

Two nights before, in a fit of temper, Rita had picked up a butcher knife and rammed it into her husband's heart, killing him.

What simple words, "Forgive us our debts as we forgive our debtors." Yet how do you forgive someone who has killed your son, your brother, your cousin, your friend, or your dad in cold blood just because she was angry?

The problem with principles of theology is that they sound easier to do than they are. Imagine being encouraged to forgive a person who has just killed someone you love! Try to comprehend the overwhelming reality of what this might entail, compared to merely giving assent to a religious slogan.

In truth, forgiveness *is* essential. But forgiveness is a *decision*, not a feeling. It is a state of mind. But as such, it does not wash away the remnants of hurt, bitterness, anger, fear, loneliness and other human responses that linger. To expect that forgiveness will wipe the slate clean is unrealistic.

Always and forevermore, those bereaved and offended survivors and victims will carry the scars of the offense. It will never go away for them.

Never will that mother embrace her son, because his wife stole his life in a fit of rage. Never will the two boys enjoy the company of their dad or hear his advice in their growing up years because mom slashed that possibility to death right before their eyes in the kitchen! Never will that mom be available to her boys because, in her act of stupidity, she also forfeited her freedom to mother them. She would spend most of the rest of her life in prison as a consequence of her behavior.

That Rita was a victim in her own way was as clear as anything. A host of psychological reasons can be authentically offered for the tragedy. But nothing changes the truth: Rita murdered her husband in front of her children.

ABSENCE OF GOD

There may be no pastoral task more difficult than that of offering crisis care to persons who feel completely forsaken by God. This sense of alienation is a part of the faith experience, however, and an unfortunate consequence of some of life's horrid moments. When we need desperately to feel close to God, we may experience only emptiness. Even Jesus cried out in anguish from the cross, "My God, my God, why have you forsaken me?"

In these moments of anguish, chaplains are called to offer care. While it may be true that for those of us who are Christian chaplains there was only one, true incarnation of the holy in the person of Jesus the Christ, nevertheless, as we all encounter others caught in the anguish of life, we participate in incarnational moments, trying to be an expression of the same God who, just now, seems so far away.

In our own ways, all of us have encountered the hard question of where God is in the depths of our human misery. As pastors, we want to proclaim the good news that God is a caring, ever-present reality. Police chaplaincy causes us to face the painful reality that the God we worship is sometimes hidden and, if known at all, it is because one has learned to "see through a glass dimly" to the God who is known more by faith than fact. And sooner than later, we must eventually come to see that in times of human sorrow God is not a magician ready to magically rescue us, but one who is willing to mourn with us. And we will likely only know this truth if there is another human being willing to sit with us in our time of distress.

*****

The over-turned pick-up still smoldered and the charred re-mains of the truck were hot from the fire. From the puddles of water that surrounded the vehicle, mists of steam rose like early morning fog. On top of the truck the upside-down cattle trailer sat precariously on its side, threatening to tumble down at any moment.

In the middle of the intersection of two country dirt roads, two horridly burned victims lay on stretchers as the paramedics worked to stabilize them. In my mind, the two burned victims seemed to be stretched out in their agony on a giant cross. Swirls of sand mixed with pieces of field debris as the first Life Watch helicopter from Wichita set down in an adjacent field. I stood in horror next to the state trooper: "Where's the second helicopter?" he pleaded on his radio. "Both these men are critical and we need those copters im-mediately! Get here now!"

Even in emergency moments as frenzied as this, sometimes there is nothing to do but stand by and wait until the next phase of care can begin. Such moments are a chaplain's precious time, they afford an opening to take in the meaning of the whole event, and sift and sort the pieces into some reality that can be grasped. For me it was not about "making sense" of the event—such hell has no sense to it at all. Still, it was always critical to prioritize issues: Who will need care later? Which caregivers seem most wounded? Did anyone personally know the victims? If so, they may need care first. Are there survivors who need attention now? Do the officers need another "authority" for crowd control? Is there a need for someone to help lift a stretcher? What natural caregivers (such as pastors, friends, or family members) need to be contacted? Is it certain that all the victims have been accounted for? Is there a need for additional searching along the ditches or around the still hot, burned-out truck? Or maybe it is enough to stand next to your good friend, the state trooper, and listen as he says, "This is the worst damn tragedy I've ever seen. I played football with John. He's not gonna make it. He's burned all over. Why can't he just die now?"

Such terrible events also provide an occasion to get a grip on yourself. After all, it's likely that you have never been this close to such human agony before. At that pitiful moment, I was standing next to the most dreadful event I had ever witnessed. I had the sense of having stumbled into hell itself. The pitiful moans of the victims, soft though they were, seemed to have a pitch of their own and nothing drowned them out. The desperate pleading of one of the victims still haunts me. "Oh my God! Please put me to sleep! Please put me to sleep!" he begged. Sometimes you need a moment to caress your own soul and reassure yourself that, beyond this agony, there will be another, better day.

From amid the gathering crowd a middle-aged farmer pushed his way toward the trooper yelling, "Hey, that's my nephew! He's got a wife at home and a little girl, too! You gotta go get them and bring them here. Now! Right now I say!"

The wide-eyed anguish of an uncle who looked onto the blistered body of his kin and who understandably saw no farther than to care for his family stood before us in trembling horror. "I understand your concern, sir," the trooper replied, "but you'll need to check with the chaplain, here. Notification is his responsibility." Truth is, it would have been easy enough for the trooper to take charge. Law enforcement personnel are used to taking charge. It is part of their personality make-up and within their demands of the job. People expect it and it seems natural.

K-58 could have taken over and he would have done well, but he gave that task to me.

When the farmer turned in my direction I answered with as much compassion and clarity as I could, "I'm so sorry, sir, but please understand we have *two* critically injured people. There's another injury in addition to your nephew. We have to know for certain that they're going to be airlifted to Wichita. We don't want to bring their families to Wichita if they aren't going there. I know it's an urgent moment, but try to understand we have to know a destination. At that point, I will personally notify all who need to know."

It seemed to take forever for the patients to be transferred, but crisis time so often seems to crawl. At last both patients were loaded into the helicopters and flown to a burn center in Wichita. With the destinations determined, I went with a trooper to notify the families of the victims.

Even years later when I drove by that intersection I remembered that lives were lost there. It always reminded me to take nothing for granted, because tomorrow is never guaranteed.

FORGIVENESS

From childhood on we learned the words and they roll with deceptive ease from our tongues. We pray, "And forgive us our debts as we forgive our debtors" (Matthew 6:12). Perhaps nothing in all the Christian faith is more essential than this. The promise is that, regardless of our transgressions, God stands ever ready to forgive us, even as we agree to forgive those who wrong us. But, like so many theological abstractions, it is easier to express than to live, because it is ever so much more difficult to do than it seems.

Saint Paul clearly understood the complexity of the human condition when he wrote, "The good I want to do, I don't; the evil I don't want to do, I do." All of us, at one time or another, have stood on either side of this dilemma—needing to be forgiven for our evil acts, even as we are called to forgive those who harm us. Forgiveness challenges us spiritually and psychologically.

***

The heavy door slammed shut with the unforgiving sound of steel against steel. Once inside, with the door tightly secured, I felt a sense of overwhelming loneliness. The inside of a county jail is another world. Built according to the contemporary standards of fifty years ago, the Harvey County Kansas jail had long since faded into an antiquated and dreary place. It would be years before the new jail replaced the old facility where my encounter with Jack took place.

Just inside the security door, I heard the staccato sound of cards being shuffled. Inmates were talking. A TV was on. A toilet flushed. With nothing soft to soak up the sounds, they bounced off the concrete floor like hail off a car in a summer thunderstorm. I walked down a short corridor past the seclusion cells, then turned east along a dimly lit catwalk by the large cell block.

The walkway was dark. Inside the cells, some inmates passed the time playing cards. Others slept on iron bunks with thin mattresses. A few nodded to greet me, having grown accustomed to my Friday afternoon visits. Sometimes they would come to the iron bars and talk with me. An exposed steel toilet conveyed a fundamental truth about life in a county jail: it is cold, unforgiving, public, exposed and hard. There is no privacy here.

Every Friday for fifteen years I made my pastoral rounds seeking to be available to inmates who might choose to confide in me about some aspect of their incarcerated lives. More often than I expected, I developed a pastoral relationship with some of them. Sometimes a sense of guilt or shame undergirded their willingness to visit with me. Maybe it was desperation. Maybe it was even an authentic sense of regret for their misdeeds. Maybe it was a need to make amends. It was pretty easy to tell the difference.

The first time I saw Jack was at his pastor's request. Jack had about the shortest temper I had ever witnessed in anyone; he seemed to have no sense of self control. And if that wasn't enough to destine him to a life of incredibly bad decisions and painful consequences, he was also driven by whatever impulses rose up from the seething mass of raw feelings that lay just below the surface of his life.

Believing that his wife was unfaithful, Jack took his revolver from his glove box one Sunday evening, walked into their home where his wife sat on a sofa between their two daughters as they watched TV, and shot her to death. It was that simple. "And that necessary, too," Jack said to me. After all, "She deserved to die for cheating on me." He had his own sense of direct justice.

The family's pastor was furious with Jack and refused to see him, so he called me. Unlike parish ministry where the congregants are typically decent citizens leading basically ordinary lives—with families, a mortgage, a job or maybe two, a few kids and a lot of Little League games and school concerts to attend—the congregation of the law enforcement chaplain is likely to include inmates in the county jail; congregants with deeply troubled souls who have never fit well into society. These men and women are often society's outcasts and are mostly unwanted.

While it took time to establish a pastoral relationship with Jack, he opened himself up to me, for reasons I will never completely understand. Never once did he deny his crime. In fact, he readily shared his story even when I encouraged him to be judicious in his confessions. I could not promise the security of a confessional since that was not part of this ministry.

The reality of confession is a complicated matter. A legal definition—such as "confessing" one's guilt in a crime—inevitably leads to a legal disposition of the matter. But confession also includes a theological perspective—"confessing" one's sins with the hope that a contrite heart and asking for God's forgiveness will allow for reconciliation with God. Both sides of the matter have merit, but they usually stand independently of each other. Obviously, one may confess and receive God's forgiveness even though he or she must still accept the legal consequences of their action. A pastoral confession does not necessarily resolve the legal complications of a crime.

Confessing and having a contrite heart never mattered to Jack.

I was struck by his understanding of God, grace, and forgiveness. "God *will* forgive me for what I've done," Jack said confidently about a month into our visits. "It's God's *job* to forgive people." It was that simple. However bad he had been—and in Jack's mind it remained an open question because of his belief that his wife was unfaithful and deserved her fate—it didn't matter. God would forgive him because, "That is God's job." I had the strange sense that Jack thought he could do anything and God would have to forgive him. That's probably true, ultimately, but only if one has a contrite and penitent heart, acknowledges the errors of his ways, and makes appropriate changes. That part, Jack never understood.

The months passed and the dreary confinement of the county jail weighed heavily on him. One afternoon, Jack seemed more subdued without his usual bravado. I wondered if he even noticed the difference. But I did. His confidence seemed muted. His certainty, mellowed. But it was the tell-tale shift in his theology that seemed most remarkable. Standing behind the iron bars by the exposed steel toilet in the darkness of the jail, Jack said pensively, "I *think* God will forgive me for what I've done." I wondered if he noticed this subtle but significant shift.

It was tempting at the outset to share Jack's theological belief that God would forgive him. Forgiveness is essential to believers. All of us have sinned and stand in need of forgiveness. But asking for forgiveness must be grounded in a life-changing and contrite heart. For me, this change in the wording of his assertion was the first authentic clue that Jack was taking seriously his inappropriate behavior, even though I don't think he recognized it as such.

Nearly a year passed during which Jack spent his time in the county jail mostly by himself. Being in jail means having time alone with your shame and guilt and the memory of what you have done. For Jack, there was no escape from his past. Every waking moment of his life included a memory of the horrible act he committed. He could still hear his daughters' screams as he shot their mother. He could still see them wipe the blood stains off themselves and watch his wife as she slumped between them.

One day, Jack waited his turn to visit with me in the dark corner of the cell block. As usual, a TV was on and inmates were playing cards. Standing before me behind the iron bars, Jack was trying to steal a moment of privacy in this hard and unforgiving place.

"Do you think God can forgive me for what I've done?" he softly asked. His voice was barely above a whisper as if he were afraid of my answer.

In the time I worked with Jack he moved from a sense of false certainty about God's forgiveness down into the valley of uncertainty. His early confidence gave way to a dreadful doubt. But in so doing, he moved from cheap grace to a recognition that he had to repent and change his heart as well as his life. As hard as it was, it seemed to serve a redemptive purpose.

There is no happy ending to Jack's story. He remained impulsive and reckless to the end. One day, he found a bottle of toxic toilet cleaner used by a trustee and drank the entire contents. The caustic cleaner burned his throat and stomach into a raw mass of open wounds with its acidic poison. For days he lingered, under guard at a local hospital, unable to talk and in great misery until he died.

"He got what he deserved," a lot of folks said. But I don't think so.

Chaplains often see the shadow side of life. We work with people who are brutally flawed and have no direction. I cannot judge Jack's life. That was up to the court system and to God. That he committed an unspeakable crime and devastated the lives of his wife and children is undeniably true. The only thing I believe I can claim is that Jack changed from an arrogant person with a superficial understanding of forgiveness to one who learned how to hope for God's grace and mercy. I think that, for the first time in his life, he faced the consequences of his behavior; he saw how absolutely in need of forgiveness he was, and how he could receive it. But always he remained trapped inside his own flawed personality.

Such an event illustrates the hidden sorrow, sin and pain which occur inside one local county jail. Because such places are not easily accessed by the public, these events may remain hidden. Inmates are not any community's best citizens and, for many of us, having them locked up simply means they aren't on the streets raising hell.

Still, it remains proper for the faith community to consider ways to provide for these errant and incarcerated people regardless of their legal problems. The biblical injunction (Matthew 25:36-39) to visit those in jail is reason enough to include them in our care.

Life will never be the same for any of those involved. But forgiveness allows the forgiver to let go of the event so that it is less present, allowing it to fade into a distant memory.

Forgiveness is a letting go of the claim that the offending person and the event has on us. The after effects will always be a reality, but the link with the perpetrator can be set aside through forgiveness. Forgiveness also lets go of the choice for retribution. The feeling that some punishment is deserved is probably a reality; the active seeking of it can be released through forgiveness. There are even occasions when people who have been hideously offended by someone can, apparently, not only forgive but continue to be in relationship with the offender. If it happens, that is a blessing. But to assume such a condition is the norm for forgiveness is naïve.

Forgiveness is a starting over—the possibility of setting aside one's bitterness to the degree that a "new normal" can be found. And as much as anything, forgiveness is an acknowledgement that some wretched event has occurred and its shattering power has forever changed your life. What helps is an acknowledgement that only God can ever adequately intervene. Our forgiveness is a recognition that we turn over to God what we cannot completely heal, and it is a willingness to let God determine ultimate consequences. That determination is not our task, however wounded we may be.

Forgiveness is reserved for those occasions in which something of grave consequences has occurred. Anything short of this simply requires an apology—we were offended, our feelings were hurt, and we need the other to say, "I'm sorry." Or vice versa: we have offended someone else. Saying or hearing "I'm sorry" helps. But apologies are a tepid response when the act is so great that the wounded one is devastated. In these times, only forgiveness works.

PRAYER

Clergy enter into intense human moments with the tradition of the church's wisdom and experience behind them. There are many pastoral responses—such as praying, referring people to other professionals, anointing the sick, listening, or worshipping—that have been applied through the years. We do well to remember them all, to know how and when to use them, but also to avoid seeing them as magic. Take prayer, for instance.

Prayer works. An historic, faith-full response, prayer acknowledges our need to turn to God in time of difficulty as well as our natural inclination to be thankful and appreciative when we are blessed.

If life teaches nothing else, it confronts us with our human limitations. We remain finite beings trying to be in relationship with the infinite. We do this through prayer as we reach out to this all-knowing, all-powerful being, seeking a blessing because just now we have reached the end of our human abilities. Law enforcement chaplains consistently work with people for whom prayer is their only hope. We regularly deal with people who are at the end of life, or overwhelmed with guilt or grief, and who seem to have no human abilities left to meet their crises. In such times, they reach out, seeking a pastoral prayer.

***

"Nine-sixteen, what's your 10-20?" asked the dispatcher..

"Twelfth and Meridian," came the deputy's reply.

"Nine-sixteen, I need you to back 909 at an unknown disturbance one-half mile north of the interstate on K15 on the east side. This is a Signal 4 [suicidal] subject and this is her parents' home.

Nine-o-nine served divorce papers on her earlier today. She's pretty Signal 4 right now and she's known to sometimes be Signal 1 [armed and dangerous] with a knife."

That cryptic message on my scanner seemed routine enough. Because the location was only a half mile from my home, and 916 was a good five miles away, I decided to respond myself. It'd give me a chance to try out my new Dodge Ram on the country roads and be available if help was needed.

Funny how sometimes the presenting incident is only a small part of a much larger one. The distraught woman was indeed at her parents' home and she *was* upset; believing them to be favoring her soon-to-be-ex-husband at her expense, she was demanding they listen to her. But there's more to this story. While 909 dealt with the persons involved, I stood in the crisp night air with 916 who arrived a few moments after me.

"Hey Rev," he began. "I need to talk to you for a minute."

"OK, Wayne. What's up?" I replied

"Seeing as how you're close to the Big Man, maybe you can put in a good word for me."

For a second, I was caught off guard. Who was the "Big Man" Wayne was talking about? Sometimes the sheriff is called "The Old Man" or "Dad" and sometimes the expression is used to refer to God, but I didn't know which it was this time? I wondered if he had a spiritual issue or was in some kind of trouble with the sheriff.

"Well, tell me some more," I asked. "What kind of 'word' do you need?"

"It's my son. He had his left hand damn near blown off yesterday at work. He works in the oil patch out near Garden City and some defective blasting cap blew up when he was getting it ready. Blew his two littlest fingers clean off and cut his thumb. But they believe they can save it."

"Oh, man!" I exclaimed. "That's terrible! I'm real sorry to hear about that."

"Yeah, well, thanks. He's had a specialist look at it and they're gonna do surgery tomorrow. They're gonna attach that hand to his stomach so it can heal. Ain't that something?"

"You bet."

"Anyway, I'm gonna catch four or five hours sleep tonight then go out first thing tomorrow morning. I ain't much at this praying business, but it's my kid, Rev. Would you pray for him?"

"I promise, Wayne, I promise."

Little things like this often matter most. Maybe Wayne's son would have done just as well without my prayers. Still, it was important for him to take me aside and ask for help. Life is made up of ordinary people who experience extraordinary moments, and who, if you have established the right kind of rapport, will let you in on the majesty of these everyday events.

There is something inherent in the office of chaplain that transcends us. It is not magic. A chaplain's work is not like the authority connected to medicine or law, which society sanctions to carry out certain rituals with power and prestige. Likely as not, what we offer will come about incidentally—on a farmhouse driveway, on a cool spring evening—when people just "happen" to talk about what's important to them. Hidden in the middle of routine incidents are the buds of hope and faith that a troubled person can't bring to life by himself.

III
PASTORAL IMPLICATIONS FOR EMERGENCY MINISTRY

The first thing any clergy seeking to provide a ministry in an emergency setting needs to remember is that *this is not our world*. It is the world of cops, lawyers, judges, jailers, probation officers, inmates, chiefs, sheriffs and paramedics. It includes people who are suddenly and wretchedly victimized and are maimed in body and soul, as well as those who have done the wounding. The language is that of rage and insult more than grace and salvation. The language is coarse and sometimes offensive. Into this thicket of despair some of us seek to enter and provide pastoral care.

The wounded ones of this world need the technical skills of a whole host of secular professionals ranging from lawyers, to judges, to physicians, to paramedics. Often the thought that they need pastoral care is not even entertained. After all, likely as not, from their perspective, they need a bail bondsman, not a pastor. They want a sharp lawyer, not a preacher. They grasp for the skills of a paramedic, not the quiet presence of a chaplain. They also need a measure of luck and courage.

Chaplains need to understand all of this. Clergy may be *allowed* in these places, but they do well to remember they are always strangers in a foreign land. Our home base is the church, not the jail or squad car or accident scene. This is not at all to imply that pastors do not belong in such settings. In fact, my conviction and claim is that pastors *ought* to be present in just those moments. Nevertheless, they need to know *how* to be present in appropriate ways.

This need for an appropriate presence is the proverbial blessing in disguise. Because the emergency scene is not our world, it forces us to seek clarity within ourselves in fundamental ways. The familiarity of working in the church too often lets us take things for granted. When we must define more clearly who we are, what we are about, what we offer and why, we are much more effective and confident.

In crisis work, the seduction that clergy face is that other professionals appear to have the most exciting and worthy things to give. They are the ones with the licensed and socially-sanctioned skills that the deeply troubled need. Clergy, with little secular blessing at all, often feel themselves to be onlookers, and may therefore lust after the skills of other caregivers. *Oh, to be a lawyer, an officer of the court, or a psychologist with a state license!*

For this reason, clergy too often set aside their own identity and grab for someone else's. They may try to be therapists, educators, cops, rescue workers, and social workers. To be sure, all these identities are worthy, but they belong to someone else.

I suspect that the seduction of wanting to be task-oriented—like a paramedic or a cop—is precisely because it is easier than to personally encounter a grieving or injured person. Clearly, legal and medical tasks are essential. But clergy can offer the skill of being focused on the individual, the situation, the rescue workers, and the families waiting to know that their lives have been altered forever.

***

We climbed over the gate and dropped to the other side. Wayne turned to me as I looked about in amazement. "Well, here it is. Hard to believe, isn't it?" he said. The old property was covered with marijuana plants. Most of the stalks were twice my height. "Ain't this something!" he said, more as a statement than a question. "We'll watch for awhile. It's a perfect place to nab 'em. Only one way in and when we know they're here, we'll be ready." He grinned as he spoke. Wayne was eager for the moment. And so we waited. Work with a county deputy suits me. I like being alone with a friend. And I enjoy the back country patrols where deer dart between the hedge rows as we pass, and where old buildings stand in silence still holding yesterday's secrets in their empty walls. It offers time to spin yarns and tell tall tales. Sometimes, it is an occasion to share a confidence: secrets that gnaw away in your heart, and which you can't … or don't … talk about. But out in the country it seems easier to talk and trust that someone will honor your story.

After several hours with no returning suspects we left the abandoned house and the stillness of the countryside and worked a couple of county blacktops, finally making our way to US 50. Wayne eventually broke the silence. "I got this new tape, Tom," he said, putting a cassette into the car stereo. "I want you to listen to it and when it's over, you tell me which song you think fits me. One of them seems written just for me." I agreed, and for awhile we rode in silence with only the sound of the radar unit interrupting the music.

I guessed Wayne was going to run some stationary radar while we listened to his tape, so we pulled onto the shoulder of the eastbound highway and parked. I let the music fill my mind and felt the pleasant summer night slowly settle over the prairie. I was still trying to figure out which song was the one which told his story.

All at once, my reveries were broken. Wayne suddenly leaned his head on the steering wheel and groaned. His breathing was thick and heavy. "Wayne, are you OK?" I asked, knowing that he had collapsed once with chest pains on a golf course. "Yeah," he said through clenched teeth.

"Let me call an ambulance!" I offered.

"Nah! I'll be OK. Probably just this hiatal hernia again." That seemed logical. After all, the earlier scare had turned out to be a painful, but non-lethal condition. "Just stress-related," he told me. But even so, I felt dread seeing my partner slumped over the steering wheel of his patrol unit, with measured, heavy breaths and silently groaning.

I knew Wayne wanted to maintain control and dignity and didn't want the ambulance called. I wondered how much I should respect his wishes. Maybe I should take control. Worried for my friend, I again offered to get help.

"Oh no," he responded. "It'll pass."

But it didn't. Wayne's face grimaced and he twisted his shoulders in pain.

"Wayne, you're in charge," I asserted. "But at least let me drive you in."

"Are you sure you can do that?" he asked, at last.

It's not easy being a cop. The personality type and the attitude are both a blessing and a curse. Independent and self-reliant to a fault, cops are *can do* people who don't easily admit to the need for help. That attitude sometimes hinders good judgment.

I walked around the patrol unit to get into the driver's seat. As Wayne rounded the back of the car, another surge of pain jolted him and he fell back onto the vehicle.

I wondered if I were giving Wayne too much space for his own choices. Maybe he needed help more than control. Still, he insisted on waiting. No ambulance yet. I tried to assist him as he walked unsteadily to the passenger's side. A passing motorist slowed, seemed ready to stop, but moved on by.

Once in the car, his pain seemed to ease. I again urged that we stop by the hospital.

"Nah, it's coffee time. Let's see how that goes first," he said. Deciding not to argue, I agreed, knowing we would only be a few blocks from the hospital anyway. And besides, I thought, maybe 915 would talk some sense into him.

As we neared the restaurant, another surge of pain stabbed Wayne. "OK Rev, you win," he said at last. "Let's go to the hospital."

Cops and physicians each have their own turf and the rules are different. Each one rules in their own realm and Wayne was now in a new domain. As they wheeled him into the emergency room, I called dispatch to notify the sheriff and to request 915 to meet me at the hospital. The rules had changed.

Being sick is scary. For a while, one lingers in a twilight of uncertainty: *Is this a serious threat to one's health and well-being? Or just a warning that you are a mortal and someday it will be deadly, though not tonight, please God.* And, all the signs of your identity are stripped away—the person who came in is transformed into "a patient." I stood by while his Beretta came off, then his shirt, his badge, his boots. His keys, too, were taken away, as well as his radio. My partner, the deputy, became my friend, the patient.

I gathered his equipment and placed it safely in the trunk of his patrol car. I was grasping onto the thought that this was just a repeat of his earlier false alarm. But gnawing away was the truth I meet each day in my work as a hospital chaplain: all of life is fragile and will end in its own time. That reality is not something we can control; we simply meet it when it confronts us.

The sheriff, the undersheriff, and other deputies came in one by one. Wayne's wife and daughter were summoned as well.

Cops and docs both live at the edge of life, a step away from destiny. It's hard to believe that the suffering we witness in the lives of others will one day be our own, so we detach from it.

As I drove Wayne's patrol unit back to his home, I felt unsettled. The early report was good. No heart damage, just his stress-aggravated condition flaring up again. But the deeper truth disturbed me, touching an awareness that I know intellectually, but rarely embrace emotionally. Namely, that there is an unknown destiny, in the darkness, that each one of us faces, and into which all of us will one day tumble. And it will come too soon. On this night I was confronted with the reality that life can take a turn in the twinkling of an eye. Often there are no warnings. The joys I know can instantly turn to dread and leave me breathless.

I would leave this moment, have coffee with the guys, and we would turn this event into one more story. But I would also know more clearly how close to the darkness we really stand.

PASTORAL PRESENCE

To work in specialized settings is to work among other professionals who are task oriented. Such professionals are used to working with victims whose lives are significantly disrupted. These people present themselves to caregivers, and caregivers then seek to apply the magic of medicine on them. This magic often works and people do get better.

Specialized caregivers tend to be problem solvers. They have a knack for focusing on problems and fixing them. This attitude is a natural product of a cultural value that prizes a "can do" spirit. Furthermore, our cultural attitude is that issues are to be solved in thirty- or sixty-minute time frames.

It is, therefore, difficult for clergy to enter an event in which there are deeply troubled people and have to stand by offering support while the other caregivers go about their tasks with precision. Sometimes such "standing by" all seems so superficial by comparison.

But not all human problems can be fixed. There are occasions in which being present and caring is, itself, a redemptive act. The pastoral care focus of emergency ministry offers the pastor an opportunity to learn more profoundly what it is like for him- or herself to encounter a person in crisis. Indeed, it is a blessing that someone else is doing the vital tasks. The pastor's responsibility is not to *do* anything so much as it is to seek an authentic human encounter, and to re-present the hope that one's faith tradition provides.

There is no more worthy human act of care than to be in authentic relationship with another. But beware. When we open ourselves to the truth of another's life, such intimacy can be painful.

AN ODD MINISTRY
"Newton to 920."

"Go ahead, Newton."

"Nine-twenty, need you to respond to West Park. The subject you were out with earlier today has returned. He's intoxicated and we're getting calls from other campers. His language is abusive and he's threatening them. They're afraid for their children's safety."

"Ten-four. En route from 12th and Meridian."

"Ten-four, 920. Be advised the park ranger has been notified, but he'll wait for you."

"Ten-four. Newton."

It could hardly have been a better summer evening. The typical July heat wave was sidetracked by a cool front and the prairie was fresh. The sun was sinking into the edge of the horizon and I could hear the sound of locusts buzzing. I was riding with 920 as I had on many of my Saturday night reserve tours, and had grown to like him as a friend and respect him as a deputy. It's funny how that goes. He's much younger than I am—about the same age as my oldest child—but that has not prevented us from building a good relationship.

That doesn't always happen. Some officers are private and don't want reserves riding with them. And for some, age makes a difference. They see me as an old man and don't know how to relate. They sense a generation gap that seems unbridgeable and that sometimes raises barriers too difficult to overcome. Others see clergy as a moral censor and fear they will be judged on something in their life. But with Scott, this was never a problem. It's hard to know, sometimes, what kindles a friendship. But in this case, it just happened. "The right front seat is always open for you, Rev," he says almost every time I close my shift.

Less than a year ago, I officiated at Scott's wedding. Chaplains are frequently called upon to offer this service. Sometimes, the couple is not connected with a faith group, yet wants a traditional wedding. I see it as an opportunity for a meaningful ministry, and I often think of the department like my parish—albeit an odd one that has its own peculiarities.

As we rode west on Twelfth Street with dusk settling over the prairie, 920 gave some direction about the situation we would be encountering.

"This guy was drunk this afternoon when I told him he needed to leave the campground. He had a friend to drive him home. He was verbally abusive to his wife and he was raising hell with other campers. He's not very big—about your size—but he's drunk and he's wiry."

As he spoke, 920 learned forward and unclasped his handcuffs from his belt and gave them to me.

"Take these. I don't expect trouble, and you don't need to get involved but if I have to fight him, I want you to get the cuffs on him as best you can."

I held the cuffs in my hand. I hoped it wouldn't come to that, but if it did, I was prepared to do my part. It's hard to predict what may happen. Most chaplains have their own rules of conduct and boundaries of their comfort zone about what they are willing to do and what they are unwilling to do. I've always taken an open stance with all of that.

In nearly thirty years of police chaplaincy, it has rarely resulted in anything much more than pastoral care in its most traditional form. The potential for a sudden, intense involvement is always there, but it rarely happens.

When we arrived on scene, the intoxicated camper recognized 920 right away and greeted him with a barrage of obscenities. If his language was offensive and verbally abusive, it was also characteristic of an inebriated and socially limited drunk. He probably needed treatment, but first he needed to leave the camp and leave the others alone. After making the expected verbal bluffs about "kicking the deputy's ass" if he wanted to, the guy ran his mouth about how tough he was. Then he either had a momentary flight into sobriety and sanity, or he saw that the deputy was backed up by the park ranger and me, and decided the odds were against him. He sheepishly entered his friend's car and they drove off, hearing the warning from 920 that "the next time would be jail time."

And then it was over.

The rest of our shift was spent as are most shifts: patrolling the ever-deepening darkness of the prairie. A quiet night, really. One that gave way to conversation.

Police chaplaincy has its unique opportunities for ministry. It is rarely ever sacramental in nature—though upon occasion a deputy may seek me out for this. Nor is it an occasion for evangelism. That pushes a boundary that must be respected. I am not there to persuade anyone to change his or her belief system, though over the years I have had many conversations about life, its meaning, and the universal quest to discover the nature and purpose of the Almighty. But this type of exchange always comes at the initiative of the deputy, not my own.

To the layperson, listening probably seems so ordinary. After all, everyone does that all the time. But pastoral listening is different from everyday listening. One must learn to hear past the words to the silence of a broken heart: the ache of a marriage breaking apart; the shame and silent sin that festers in someone's soul; the fear of failure. This kind of listening prompts the chaplain to accompany another inside a place where all manner of difficult memories are filed, and then help to process whatever it is that stands silently in this dark night within the soul. Indeed, the police chaplain's privilege is to care for the souls of those who wear the badge. It is to listen beyond the words to the silent, unspoken concerns that are hard to reveal in ordinary times and places. But if the chaplain has built the relationships solidly enough, deep listening will allow him or her to hear the unexpressed joys or bewildering decisions that officers must make in their personal life or in the line of duty.

Police chaplaincy is a ministry of presence. It is not evangelism. It is not sacramental. It is not much of anything traditional at all. But it is always important.

THE BUILDING SEARCH

"Nine-o-nine, need you to respond to 1000 North Hoover Road. Have a citizen report that the neighbor's glass door appears broken open. All our city units are busy with the armed robbery at Dillon's Market in the city. It is unknown if there is any connection with the robbery and this call."

"Ten-four Newton," responded Dave, 909. That was the end of coffee.

I left the rest of my coconut cream pie on the plate and followed him to his car. As we traveled in silence, I watched 909 as he drove us, Code 3, through town. Lights from oncoming cars brightened his face. He would never admit it ... I probably wouldn't either, but I thought he looked worried. Not frightened, maybe just anxious.

"Nothing like a building search to get your adrenalin pumping. I love the challenge and the excitement of it all! Stay close and keep behind me. And put these in your pocket in case you need them," continued Dave as he handed me an extra set of keys to his patrol car and a snub-nosed .38 which he carries in his coat for back up. Nothing else was said, but that was enough. I knew what he meant. If he were wounded, I would need some way to have access to the vehicle and the means to cover my own safety. And it would also help him, too, in a crisis. I shuddered at the thought and then dismissed it. Though such a dreadful possibility exists, you can't think of it all the time or it will cripple your work.

I quietly shut the door, stepped over the short fence, and followed closely behind 909 as we kept to the shadows. Overhead, the autumn sky sparkled with stars. But even with the moonlight, the deep shadows darkened the background of the house and I felt my heart thump against my bullet-proof vest. My hands were sweaty as I clutched the .38 in the pocket of my dark-blue jacket with the bright yellow letters—SHERIFF—across the back.

Dave and I crossed both the neighbor's backyard and the alley, and then stopped just behind the metal tool shed, which gave us some protection for a moment. We looked all about the darkened house. Neither of us moved. I watched as Dave studied the broken, sliding glass door of the house and listened for sounds that didn't belong.

"Nine-o-nine Newton," Dave called dispatch.

"Go ahead, 909."

"Newton, give us emergency traffic only on Channel 2; 606 and I will be checking this building."

"Ten-four, 909. All units, emergency traffic only on Channel 2."

And then it was quiet. Those silent moments are important to me because it gives me a few seconds to fit things together. It's too hard to process thoughts when you have to attend to every move, every sound. Nine-o-nine checked the lock on the shed to make sure it was secure so no one would hit us from behind when we left it. We crept toward the house.

Dave pulled his .9mm from his holster and motioned me to follow. I could hardly believe I was going into a building one more time to look for possible intruders. After all, we were both fifty years old! Dave and I had joked about this fact all the time. At our age, searching darkened buildings makes you think about the span of your life and what matters most to you. Everything looks different for us now. Even the most ordinary things confirm the truth of mortality. We can't escape our hair turning gray, for example, and although I run three miles every day, it takes longer each year, and sometimes I ache more than I used to. There are more yesterdays than tomorrows for both of us, and each tomorrow seems shorter and costs us more.

We silently approached the shattered sliding glass door, stood to the side of it, and peered intently into the blackness of the empty house. Could it be that the armed robber from Dillon's Supermarket had sought refuge in this darkened, deserted house? There seemed no way to know except to search the place, room by room. As Dave stepped on shards of glass, I was surprised at how I cringed at the loud crunch. What if our security had been betrayed? What if any hidden intruder would be forewarned?

Stepping into the doorway, I strained to see, but the darkness closed around us like a thick prairie fog. I opened my mouth so I could breathe more quietly. I remember how Dave once said that in dark places like this he listens intently for the heavy breathing or nervous moving of hidden intruders. He even tries to sniff the air for the faint scent of aftershave. I felt a little silly, but there I was, listening and sniffing as if I knew what I was doing.

Suddenly, Dave pressed his flashlight on, for a small piece of a second, and the kitchen was illuminated. Its dark secrets—nothing but remodeling debris—were laid bare, and we continued through the hall into the living room.

Though still dark, enough moonlight shown through a window for me to see. Dave motioned me to crouch down and we peered around an entrance into the living room. Once more, the darkness was split in brilliance as Dave switched on his halogen light. There was no one there.

Old paint cans littered one corner … A rumpled drop cloth covered the floor near a freshly painted wall … A four-foot step-ladder, all splotched with paint, stood upright waiting to be used again. But that was all.

How bizarre all this was! Not far away, Newton units were looking for an armed robbery suspect while Dave and I were winding our way, room by room, through an empty house. I didn't feel fear so much as wariness. *Someone* had broken in, but when? Were they still hidden in some dark corner? If so, perhaps it was only a drifter wanting a warm place on a cool autumn night. Or maybe it *was* the armed robber from Dillon's.

Suddenly, I heard a faint crack from upstairs. Nothing certain. Nothing clear. Just a sound. I swallowed, feeling my hands grow wet with sweat. Dave pointed to the staircase and we crept up, slowly, silently.

"Probably just the normal creaking of an old house," I thought to myself. After all, my own knees creak when I climb the stairs. I shuddered as I remembered a recent tragedy in Wichita in which the police, trying to protect a home that had been previously bur-glarized, had shot someone who was house-sitting. I felt the weight of that memory and put the thought out of my mind. I needed to be attentive to *this* moment and to *our* task. What would I do if *this* silent work suddenly turned vicious? I shuddered at the thought.

Once upstairs, we found a single room. In the far corner, a clos-et. Dave pointed first to me, and then to the doorknob, indicating that at his signal I was to yank the door open.

For a moment it all seemed so real and yet so bizarre, with images of every cop movie I had ever seen. I felt foolish. Even so, as I reached for the doorknob I felt the specter of life and death hover about the darkened room. If an intruder were in there, opening that door would surely mark a moment of destiny for all of us. It was the longest second I had ever known. But the closet was empty.

I was at the edge of anxiety with my feelings, while Dave seemed beyond his own stress and looked calm. I felt fully *in* the moment, even while I was somehow off to the side watching us both within this highly charged experience.

Dave's flashlight shattered the darkness as we peered inside the closet. A few coat hangers ... nothing else. The building was empty.

"Nine-o-nine, traffic for Newton."

"Go ahead, 909."

"You can resume normal radio traffic on two. The building is secure; 606 and I will be back in service."

But just as a memory lingers long after a cherished moment passes, the truth of that evening holds fast in my mind. In our own ways, each of us stood closer than we felt comfortable to that lonely place where life and death seem intertwined.

The Chaplain's Notebook
Part I: General Principles for Working with Cops

If you seek an alliance with law enforcement, I believe there are some general principles for a chaplain to follow to adequately prepare him- or herself for effective pastoral work.

1. Establish a solid trust level with the officers. It is very difficult to create a useful working alliance right away. Law enforcement is a close-knit group, and finding acceptance is no easy task. It is hard to jump onto a fast-moving train; getting on board early is much better. Waiting for them to call you usually means a long wait. Chaplains need to take initiative, become known and find ways to establish rapport. Officers are extremely reluctant to have a stranger beside them in moments when there may be conflict. They ask themselves privately, "Can I trust him? Can I count on him? Will he know what to do? Will I have to take responsibility for him?" These are the kinds of concerns that must be faced before trust is established. Until a chaplain earns a place, he or she will likely be an outsider.

2. Find ways to build a liaison with duty officers. Taking the time to truly enter their world is useful. Riding with officers on patrol or being a part of law enforcement organizations (if permitted) is helpful. Being at the department and drinking coffee so as to be known and to know them also helps. Being willing to accept the risks of patrol work is valuable. Personally, I advocate being a fully authorized reserve officer so that you show some commitment to their world and work and, therefore, have legal credibility.

3. Establish trust with administration. This is critical, and with it your work has a better chance of acceptance. One must be careful, however, that he or she is not seen as the chief's pet project or that your allegiance is really with the chief and not the duty officers.

4. Know how to hold a confidence. If line officers or the administration are to trust you, both need to be convinced that what is told to you will be held in confidence. To betray a piece of privileged communication is very likely to result in officers or administration having nothing to do with you.

5. Be available. Crisis work accepts no convenient schedule. A crisis can (and does) happen in any and all moments. One must be willing to respond when summoned. This is a special burden for chaplains. Unless you have colleagues who can share the responsibility with you, then it may be your task alone to be available immediately when the crisis occurs. It *is* disruptive to your private life. Therefore, it simply must be something you believe in enough so that you are willing to accept the responsibility and respond when called. Obviously it all works most effectively when there is a team of chaplains and the burden is shared.

6. Learn the language and procedures of law enforcement. Any profession has its unique language and law enforcement is no different. A chaplain must be familiar with whatever is policy and procedure for the department. It is a reasonably small thing to do, but it pays big dividends. Life on the streets is rough, and so is the language. Clergy need not adopt such language, but it is not helpful to carry a judgmental attitude toward every person whose language is tart and who relies on four-letter words to make their point. Being non-reactive is not the same as condoning.

7. Learn well the concepts of grief work and crisis intervention theory. This may be the one area in which you have the most significant gift to bring. Cops are expected to know police procedures. Citizens in a crisis are clearly caught up in the procedural element of the experience and it is here that officers feel "at home." The human dimension such as grief work or post-traumatic stress reaction is less familiar ground. A knowledgeable, experienced chaplain brings a critical gift to both the citizen and to law enforcement involved in the incident.

8. Accept that crisis work by definition is chaotic and upsetting. Life often exists at the edge of death. Anger boils in the hearts of victims. The very urgency of the moment demands action. Indeed, a quick response may save a life. But strangely enough, deeper than the need for another active involvement by another worker, the chaplain may well find that his or her most valued gift is a ministry of presence. A willingness to stand as witness to hope and comfort in an event where all appears lost is crucial. Being present, accepting the tears and anguish without turning away, and listening are valuable offerings. Having the ability to be present, to pay attention, to *name* the experience for what it is, are a pastor's tasks. When a pastor has been a part of crisis work on the streets, other officers and emergency workers value his or her presence because they know that the chaplain understands.

IV
PASTORAL AUTHORITY

When immediate intervention in emergency situations is not our primary work, we are forced to clarify our pastoral identity in other ways. With less "hands on" tasks—like those done by police and medical personnel—chaplains may find themselves with more opportunities to establish meaningful pastoral relationships with people in trouble. Therefore, we need to learn to claim our authority in this, our rightful domain, and act on this claim.

In such times when real relationship is called for, there is no place to hide. Clichés don't work. All we have to offer is ourselves. Nowhere have I seen more clearly the value of reaching deep down inside myself and grasping some authentic piece of who I am and offering it than in crisis ministry. Degrees and prestige do not matter. The bigger question is, can you care? Can you find a way to encounter the anguish of this moment? Can you embrace the sorrow? Can you see the faith issue that is truly there beyond the theological talk that sometimes hides the truth? Can you accept your authority and offer the accompanying word of confrontation to one who needs to face his or her shame and fear? Perhaps nothing both invites and allows a chaplain to claim and experience his or her authority as much as a disaster, when law enforcement personnel need you to claim a piece of the action and carry it out with conviction. This is the time to see what ground you've built within yourself. Is it solid enough to plant your feet on and stand firm? In the heat of the crisis moment you will be called upon to seize the presented opportunity and act, because inside yourself you know you are capable. It doesn't matter that you are or are not sanctioned to claim it; the circumstances themselves, plus your own experience, demand that you accept the responsibility. If you fail, those who need you will suffer.

The expected cautions about not over-stepping your authority and entering someone else's clearly established (and probably legally authorized) area surely apply. Still, emergencies provide ample, empty zones where pastors can claim authority because it is right to do so.

THE REAL WORK

One reason to work in emergency ministry in law enforcement and the county jail settings is to deal with the bare bones of faith. This is not like teaching Theology 101 or Intro to Pastoral Care. This work is much less conceptual and much more experiential in nature. It is symbolized in one despondent inmate who, in his moment of despair while on an errand with a cop to get some clothing from his home, grabbed a hidden gun and blew the top of his own head off. Pastoral care in this moment is attending to the ashen-faced county attorney who stands on this side of the event, so far away from the well-known and familiar security of the courtroom. It is attending to the cautious paramedic who steps gingerly over the widening pool of blood to avoid the still lethal .38. It is care to the cop who wonders if it were, indeed, his fault. It is listening to the fearful tenants, peeking from behind closed doors, who must live with the ghost of this moment lurking in the darkness of the hall. It is support for the other officer who puts his own weapon back in his holster now that he knows the shooting was self-inflicted and not done by another. And it is care for the deceased's sister in a nearby town, who sits in silent sorrow when I tell her the news. "Oh, I just knew he would do this," she says. "He was so lonely." It is me, too. One more time I stand inside the weary world of broken dreams and watch as we scrape up the loose ends of still one more raw moment of life. Pastoral care in these moments includes some level of concern for everyone involved and it deals with fundamental faith issues.

CATHERINE, LONG SINCE DEAD

Law enforcement work is sometimes so ugly, so unspeakably wretched, that it hides behind grisly humor and silence. It's an ugliness rarely known by others, and when its presence is suspected, it is as often as not left in unspoken shadows.

Winter 1985. My parents-in-law's fiftieth wedding anniversary. A cold, rainy winter day. A good day, though. One filled with friends, family, memories, and love. And lots of hard work. So by the end of the day my wife and I were worn out. She lay on the couch to read. I went to the sheriff's office to see my friends and to drink coffee. Just as I entered the squad room, my pager squealed and the detective walked in.

"Holy cow!" he says. "I page 606 and he appears just like magic! Have we got something for you!"

A silent surge of excitement burst through me when I heard this. It's so often that way. There is something seductive about working with cops … at once exciting and dramatic. I sometimes cringe at my attraction to this dark world of violence and evil. I wonder about myself. Do I really *like* the risk, or is it more that I like the reality that it affords me—a place to engage people in their most vulnerable times. Maybe both.

Honestly, I like the risk, the drama, the excitement. Long ago I learned that it's the subtle tones of voice and the teasing smirks which betray hidden truths about me that the detective knows when he says, "Have we got something for you!

"Oh, yeah? What's up?"

"Well, we found a body. That is, we found what's *left* of a body!"

"What's left of a body." A simple phrase said with a smirk. And before I can stop my wondering mind, a rush of curiosity floods inside of me. I've never seen "what's left of a body" and some macabre curiosity stirs deep within … My dark side?

For reasons perhaps never to be completely known, a young woman died in her basement apartment. A woman whose body is now so completely melted away by time and chemistry that visual identification is impossible. Even so, it is necessary to find some way to make a positive identification so that the family of this dead woman can know that evil truth. Together with the detective, I sat down on the floor of his office to explore the secrets of her purse, trying to put together the pieces of a puzzle of a week-old dead body found by neighbors who didn't like the foul odor in the next door apartment and called police.

Her purse contained just enough scraps left to give a hint of a life, but not enough to make anything clear. What *was* there, though, gave a clear enough clue that she led a secret life in the drug world. Illegal pills and drug paraphernalia lay tucked away in a black leather pouch in the bottom of her purse. But the real story was not fully apparent from the odds and ends—from a quick glance at a mix of pills, credit cards, keys and pieces of paper. Yes, her identification showed us her name, Catherine, but even that too was only one piece of a jigsaw puzzle, and it didn't fit.

"Well, let's go back to the apartment, Tom," the detective suggested. Maybe we'll find something else there that will give us a lead." As I slipped behind the steering wheel of my Dodge van, I remembered the stories of the old-time cops who used to joke about carrying a bottle of Noxema in their cars for just such moments. It always seemed so peculiar, but on this night I found myself wishing I had a jar just in case—just in case I wanted to smear a dab under my nose to block out the pungent stench of decaying human flesh. That's what the Noxema was for.

At the residence, I walked down the sidewalk to the back door entrance to the apartment and felt shivers run up and down my spine. I thought to myself, "I know it's dumb. I know it's only a dead body. And even if it was murder, it was a week ago. There's no danger here, now." Still, the night time shadows seemed heavier than usual, and something lurked in the stillness. I could swear that the mid-winter night seemed lifted right out of an Edgar Allen Poe story. Deep, gray clouds skidded just over the bare tree tops and oozed a cold winter mist. From time to time, breaks in the clouds teased me with yellow moon glow, which cast shadows in the night.

Another shiver crawled up my spine as I stood alone on the back steps. I took a deep breath of clean winter air and stepped through the back door. Just inside, I was assaulted by the smell of death. My eyes stung with this foul air and my stomach rolled. The stench was awful up on the back landing, but grew even heavier as I walked down.

I watched as officers methodically investigated all possible clues and uncertainties in the basement apartment.

"Go on back, if you want to, Tom. There's not much to see. They took the body away just before you came. Go take a look if you want."

"Straight back there?" I asked, not really knowing which way to turn. In the living room the cops were wearing latex gloves, going through drawers, looking underneath couch cushions and poking through old closet secrets.

"Yeah, just follow your nose. You can't miss it!" he said with a twinkle in his eye … in gallows humor jest. Even in the midst of it all, someone has something morbidly clever to say.

Once past the living room and into the kitchen, I paused and stood alone in the silence. What happened here? The kitchen table was set and a dried half-eaten pizza sat on a plate. A fork rested on the plate with scraps of old food still caked on the prongs. An empty Pepsi can lay on its side. The silence was heavy, the air was foreboding. I realized that I was afraid to breathe. Somehow it felt that, with each breath, I sucked in a piece of death itself. It was everywhere. As I moved on toward the bedroom, part of me wanted to turn around and go back to the relief of the living room where I could see life at work.

What an ironic description, "the living room." But it was true. Out there, far away from this dead bedroom that I was approaching, there were living folks searching for some piece of truth which might make this mystery seem understandable. But I was not ready, yet, to rejoin the "living" back there. There was something else I had to see. It was not easy to walk through that narrow hallway that led to the bedroom. It felt so tight. The smell of death grew more oppressive. It was silent in this hallway and in the room ahead. And so lonely. The muffled sounds of the investigation could scarcely be heard here. I was all alone with some unseen but very real presence, and far away from "the living room."

"What was it like for her, anyway, in that lonely moment?" I asked myself. "Did she take her life in a moment of despair? Did she suddenly become ill? If so, did she suffer or was it a quick exit? Was she afraid?" And maybe most awful of all, I wondered if she was murdered. And *if* that had happened, then the silence here would be more than sad: it would be evil. But, only the silence knew.

Still, I had to know what I *could* know. So, with my decision grounded on the reality that I was not really alone, I walked into the bedroom, relieved that the body itself had been removed. At least I wouldn't have to see her. I could, however, see the still dark outline of where she lay on her bed for a week. Nothing was left but vapor and stains ... and the unspoken terror of neighbors, who heard rumors that it was one of them who might be responsible. And the pale-faced cops who donned latex gloves and searched for clues. And a chaplain who knows he stands on holy ground—a place where life slipped away.

What's a chaplain to do here? Nothing ... but be present with himself and with those who breathe in death's remains. Nothing ... but share the grisly job of law enforcement. Still, it does count to share the burden: to hear the story; to breathe the stench yourself; to stand close by and be as fully present as you can to those who must do a horrid task. And to listen for some sound beyond the silence ... some word from the walls.

A SON'S DEATH

Those who have a ministry with emergency services are involved in difficult faith issues. Likely as not, many of us grew up with a Sunday School theology as the beginning point in our faith. Such a foundation is valid because it lays a solid base. But life has a way of chipping away at the simple truths of Sunday School answers. While not necessarily incorrect, they often are too simplistic for handling complex issues. The age old struggle of why God allows "bad" things to happen to "good" people is a legitimate question that deserves a thoughtful response.

***

I have learned to pause for a fraction of a second before speaking when the phone rings in the night. There is sometimes a strange but telling background noise, nothing specific, just a distinctive hollow sound that gives me the clue that it's the Harvey County communications center on the line.

"Chaplain Shane, this is 911. We've just had an accident. It's a probable fatality and the sheriff is asking for you to be notified. Can you come?" With one variation or another, this is my summons to yet one more crisis ministry moment.

Police chaplains are surely intrigued, at first, by the drama and excitement of the work. To be allowed on the scene, to be where the action is, is exciting. But that initial excitement fades quickly as the incident shifts to tragedy and one sees the depths of human suffering. Chaplains whose only interest is the adrenalin rush do not last. The reality is too overwhelming. Those who stay in police chaplaincy do so because they have discovered that there is a place for ministry in such moments, and that without some willing chaplain there, important care will not be given.

I dressed quickly, told my wife the sketchy details, and then hurried to the scene outside of town. The nighttime sky was ablaze with flashing red lights. Rescue units had set up portable generators and huge spotlights illuminated the tragedy. The traffic was blocked off a quarter mile on either side of the accident, and in the center of the flashing lights, paramedics worked feverishly to attend to the survivors. Before I approached the sheriff and the trooper standing nearby, I looked around.

A million slivers of glass covered the highway, and sparkled. Huge chunks of twisted metal lay on the highway like broken monuments to the tragedy. The jaws of life had already ripped apart one car, freeing the passengers from its grip, and they had been attended to and sent Code 3 to the hospital for further care.

My attention was drawn to the other vehicle. But at first, I actually tried to avoid looking at it. Inside was the dead body—the "10-40." Strange how we depersonalize such moments. What that car held now was not a bunch of numbers at all, but, until moments ago, a man who surely had some family and friends who loved him, and whom soon I would have to tell.

It is my job to pay attention to human feelings and behavior. Chaplains do that. I looked about as everyone carried out their work with the precision of a well oiled machine. Incredible how efficient things become in what is certainly a wretched moment of anguish for all involved! I look at people's faces, too, for they tell the stories as certainly as do their words. Sometimes I hear the macho stories of those who try to push back their own anxiety by telling jokes out of place, and I know the words are only attempts to hide the officer's feelings. Better to whistle in the dark, or to depersonalize this awful moment, than to give in to it. One must stay in control to do the job.

But in the trooper's eyes, I could see his sorrow. His look betrayed his sensitivity to the human drama. As he carried out his job of charting the accident, taking the measurements, and taking pictures, he could not mask his caring. More so than anyone, he knew that we all live at the raw edge of such moments, and that no one is immune. This could just as easily have been his family, and he knows it. This awareness colors his work with compassion.

In silence, we rode to a pleasant farmhouse and turned up the long, gravel road to the country home. The late fall night was clear, and the air still held the warmth of late summer. The sounds of night seemed strangely pleasant and serene, a tragic mockery to what had really happened.

This is the hardest part.

The old dog has already barked our presence, and even as we walk to the door, we see a light brighten in an upstairs room. The trooper knocks on the door, and we wait in anxious silence as we sense someone walking through the house to warily greet us. We can see the inhabitant peering through a side window, before opening the door. Nighttime visitors are not always friendly, and people are wary. I don't blame them. The presence of the uniformed officer and the squad car give both reassurance and dread. We may be "safe," but why have we come? As the door opens, we see a middle-aged couple standing together, as if to draw strength from each other as they wait to learn our mission. My heart beats heavily and my palms are damp with dread.

"Mr. and Mrs. Smith?" I inquire. "I'm Chaplain Shane of the Harvey County Sheriff's Department. This is Trooper Jones. We have some information for you which we must bring. Are you ready to hear us?"

I pause for a moment, watching them gain a necessary grip on their inner strength. Even in the dark of night, I see their faces draw pale in dread. Our pause is precisely designed to give them time in which to prepare themselves for the bitter news they sense is on its way.

"Mr. and Mrs. Smith, there has been an auto accident in the county. It involves your son, Ted. I am so sorry to have to tell you he was killed."

Oh how I hate to say that! Though it is not my fault, I never get used to being the bearer of such despicable news. It is so sad to see a family's world crumble to dust before our eyes. The trooper and I stand there in the warm September night and listen to the aching, empty sobs of a mother and father as they grieve their once bright promise of a son, now dead.

Hard though it is, such ministry must take place. People have a right to have this tragic news carried to them by someone willing to stand alongside them in this most empty of all moments. They have a right to a ministry that will help bring them their natural caregivers, their own religious leader, their family, their neighbors, perhaps a supervisor at work. And that is part of what chaplains do: summon, if they desire, their loved ones. We stay for as long as is proper, and leave when some measure of stability has returned.

We returned to the sheriff's office where we found some solace in a cup of hot black coffee and some personal sharing of our own feelings. It never fails to happen—the trooper or the deputy responds with the compassion of one who has been touched and enriched by being a part of a terrible tragedy. There is no joy in such moments. The hours that follow are restless ones, for we have seen the underbelly of life, its shadow side, and it takes a while to return to hope. But we have some satisfaction in knowing that a difficult job was done with compassion.

DEATH AT TWIN BRIDGES

Crisis care is full of learning moments, beyond the immediate pastoral care opportunities, that can help us to see the wider picture of the church. When the local pastor is called in, we see the power of a healing church which opens its arms to embrace one of its own, now broken in grief. It is easy to forget that we in specialized ministries are always linked to the larger faith community.

Sometimes my own pain or stress or ineptitude stands in the way of my pastoral care and I can't see clearly. Or maybe I miss something critical because I am too caught up in the drama and fail to offer a pastoral presence. Or perhaps my own excitement and desire to be involved blinds me to something pastoral and I forget my own roots and try to be something I am not—like a therapist or a cop. Maybe I am just too deeply touched by the moment—I stand too near the sorrow—and slip beyond the boundary of caution and get burned myself. Perhaps I over-function and try to rescue and, consequently, ignore proper boundaries. The extraordinary pain that comes to ordinary folks caught in such moments of horror is hard to guard against and we chaplains easily resonate with the despair.

***

Following a routine Sunday-morning religious discussion group, I sat with two students to process the experience. Midway through our session my pager went off and I was asked to call the communications center. I was told that there was a major accident with one fatality and one critical injury at Twin Bridges, at the site where US 50 and Ridge Road intersect. Each road has a bridge at the intersection but only US 50 has the right of way. I was asked to respond immediately, and told that hysterical family members were on the scene and that help was needed.

Relaying this information to my students, I gave them the option of accompanying me or staying at the hospital. One elected to go, the other stayed. We dashed to the car and were soon on our way to the trauma. The on-scene visual impact was overwhelming. The mid-day August heat was blistering and heat waves shimmered off the highway. Traffic was halted, but I snaked my way through the vehicles to get as close to the scene as possible and parked near the sheriff's car. Bystanders were annoyed at my disregarding of the deputies traffic control, but seemed calmed when I exited, wearing my sheriff's hat which I use at such times to give me credibility. My student stayed close by my side. I could see her glance at the tragedy and wince in horror. It was hot as hell, and I felt as if we might be there.

The scene was ugly. Off to the side a pickup truck sat in the ditch. The bed of the truck was caved in, where a motorcycle had rammed into it. Bits and pieces of the Harley were strewn for fifty yards in all directions. Fuel and oil slicked the highway and oozed together with flesh and blood. But ugliest, and saddest of all, were the bodies of a mother and son who lay broken and disfigured on the black asphalt. The dead son was barely recognizable as a person. The mother was alive but gravely injured; already attended to by the paramedics, she was being sent Code 3 to the hospital.

"It's a mess, Tom," the sheriff greeted me. "The old man in the truck blew the stop sign and the kid couldn't stop and rammed them. Hell of a mess. What's worse, a quarter mile behind them was the kid's sister, and she saw it too. Another sister and a son-in-law got here soon after. They're all in that motor home over there. That's where you need to go. Don't know whose home it is, but they stopped to give help and let the family members go inside for comfort."

And it was so. The endless sobs and bitter sighs of grief that echoed within the motor home brought no peace. Who knows what it is like to see your younger brother dead and your mother broken and bleeding? Two sisters and one son-in-law knew. And they wept and screamed. They all needed care: the officers who picked up the pieces; the paramedics who did their best; the old couple who meant no harm but, through their driving error, had brought death and despair to an innocent family on their way to a picnic; and even an itinerant family who opened up their mobile home to strangers who hurt so deeply. The deputies and the hospital personnel needed support too. It may have been a job for them and it may even have been the kind of trauma they had seen before. But one never gets used to seeing people disfigured or maimed and in great distress.

There was no time to do anything except make a quick assessment of who needed help most of all, and be with them. Afterwards, there was a journey to the hospital where other family members gathered to hear the same story and cry new tears.

And again, the same question: How could such a terrible event come so quickly and so finally to such good people?

What do chaplains do in such broken moments? They stand between one uncle and his niece to keep him from his own grief-born need to "knock her out so she'll stop crying." They listen to the nurses who choke back their tears "because as near as we can tell, every limb and every rib was broken in the mother," and their task was to care for this broken and critically wounded soul. Later, when a measure of calm has settled down on the small town hospital, and the hot August afternoon was once more still, chaplains will sit with the sheriff and listen to his macabre humor, which they know is a shallow cover for the ache that lives inside him at having to once more see an awful event.

A CHRISTMAS SPIRIT

The task of a chaplain is to set events in the context of a still larger picture. Theological reflection seeks to find meaning in troubled times.

***

Eight o'clock Sunday morning. Much too early for my phone to ring and push me into the day. Much too early after being out until 1:00 A.M. riding with a trooper, and then working a crisis incident as the hospital on-call person. But phones and people in crisis don't know all that.

"Chaplain Shane, it's Mrs. Jones. Do you remember me? You came to my farm seven years ago yesterday to tell me that my husband was killed in a wreck." As I sat at the edge of my bed trying to pay attention, I thought to myself, "Do I remember her? That's the wrong question. Will I ever forget?"

What sad words. Seven years ago yesterday it was a crisp, clear December night. It seemed like every star in the sky was visible in Harvey County, and that every Christmas carol being sung that night could be heard, if you listened just so. But that peaceful night seven years ago was shattered when I arrived at the scene of the accident. The rumble of the portable generator drowned out every other sound. The emergency lighting system nearly blinded me as I looked at the little Toyota which was overturned, and shattered like a Christmas tree ornament which had tumbled to the floor.

My heart pounded in my chest as I approached the Toyota. From a distance I could see the blood-stained and lifeless form of the driver slumped over the steering wheel. This was my first automobile fatality event, and I knew I needed to see it first from afar. I had to ease myself closer to the trauma to prepare myself for what I was about to see. On that day, seven years before, I was closer to raw human suffering than I had ever been. My belly felt queasy. All about me were reminders that I was walking into the dead center of a tragedy.

A few officers talked quietly to each other as they tried to figure out what might have happened. Once in a while, the crackle of someone's radio broke the constant roar of the generators. Underfoot I felt the crunch of shattered pieces of windshield as I walked ever closer to the truck. And there it all was. My breath turned to frost in the sharp cold.

That seven-year-old memory was as fresh as the morning's call. I remembered watching the rescue squad work themselves into a hot sweat on that cold December night as they cut through the second vehicle, a shattered semi. They were trying to reach the victim pinned inside that wreckage, who was known only by the moans that came from within.

I recall thinking, "How could I ever tell another what I saw?" And so I turned away, but it did no good. The reality was still there. It would not go away.

To be sure, in the incredible rush to do whatever is humanly possible to save life and relieve suffering, one finds hidden resources of strength and courage to do what later seems impossible. But, nonetheless, one is left with deep bruises to his soul. One's secret self is scarred by what he has heard and seen. Later, sleep will not come because uninvited ghosts silently stare, and haunt you with memories. You may see a vacant and disfigured face looking back at you, and you cannot close your eyes to the scene.

I know that old memories live inside and can stay quiet for a long time until summoned by something as ordinary as a phone call. Then, as the memory door opens a crack, the old memories creep out.

We're all the same: cops, troopers, deputies, fire fighters, paramedics, and chaplains. We all have ghosts that live inside us. We can pretend they aren't there, but they are.

Mrs. Jones's voice brought me back to the present. "I know I have my nerve calling you this early on Sunday, but this is just killing me. The hurting won't go away. Every Christmas it's the same. And my son, John, he's turned to drink. He never could accept his dad's death and he's so cold-hearted now; I think he died too. Please, could I make an appointment to see you? I can't stand another broken Christmas!"

We set up a time to visit, talked a little more, and I carried her pain with me for the rest of the day. Certainly I would rather have heard of Christmas cheer. But old ghosts often whisper to me when I least expect it. And perhaps the only reason for Christmas, anyway, is because of all the sad and lonely folks who sit in silence. I believe God cares enough to slip inside those moments of broken dreams and sad hearts, and tell us that there is hope and help and healing.

For many of us, Christmas is indeed trees, presents, the idea of wassail whether we drink it or not, and holiday cards. It's the wide-eyed wonder of your child as she pokes and pinches the mountain of presents under the tree. It is the warm embrace of those you love so dearly who come home because they love you too. Christmas is giggles and wonder. It is Santa Claus and fruitcake. And your children's smiles.

But for some, Christmas is the empty echo of one who is not there, of smiles no longer given, presents never unwrapped, cards not received. A lonely day because some precious one is gone, it may be the longest, most empty day of the year.

If we want Christmas to be truly a time of redemption and joy then we must look past the parties and presents. We need to listen deeper than the carols and warm greetings. We must *be* Christmas, ourselves, for those who need healing and hope. We must pray for those whose loneliness knows no end. We must cry with those whose eyes spill tears of grief, even as we laugh with our children. And always we must know for certain that God is present whenever we hold each other and offer comfort.

TANYA'S LAMENT

Chaplains represent the presence of God in the center of agony. Our lives become an incarnational theology. In the context of emergency ministry, deeper than the confusion and chaos, and undergirding the desperate questions of faith, one so often sees how the presence of God is witnessed and alive in those who care. Indeed, where two or three are gathered in Christ's name, God is present.

***

I walked into the living room, stopped and looked around, once again trying to understand who needed care first and most.

The officer motioned me to the dining room, and I stepped aside as two paramedics rolled past me with a gurney, carrying the black body bag with the dead father—brother-uncle-husband-friend—inside. I breathed a sigh of relief that he had been taken care of. Even so, the experience was troubling. From my vantage point in a corner of the room, I watched as one of the dead man's brothers dumped the bloodied sheets into a black plastic garbage bag from off the bed where his brother had shot himself to death. I peeked into the bedroom as another brother sponged bits of his beloved brother's shattered head off the wall … pieces which but moments ago contained a bizarre mix of hope and despair, of sorrow and anger, of love. My job in this moment was clear. I walked half a block away to a neighbor's home; the dead man's five-year-old daughter was waiting here and must be told. No one else, including her mother, could bring themselves to the task—to say the words that her daddy was dead. "Please help us, chaplain. Tell her for us," the other family members asked.

Can you feel the pain of overwhelming grief inside, deep down where tears are born and rage boils when life is so unfair? Entering the neighbor's living room, I saw the little red-headed child nestled under her mother's arm. I knew a truth that would wound her forever, and I would bring it home to her. She knew that something was wrong, even if she didn't know what.

To tell people that their world is shattered is a terrible task. Chaplains need to do it gently, with love and kindness. Make no mistake about it—such work wounds the teller, too. I shake inside and sweat. I rehearse the awful words I must say, but it does no good. Every event is different even if they are so similar. I see it in their eyes: they know I bear bitter news, or why else have I come?

For a moment, as I paused by the couch and knelt before the mother and child, I reached inside for a courage I wished were stronger. For a second, I saw my own five-year-old daughter in her place, and I swallowed the tears which surely arose from my soul.

"Tanya, my name is Tom. I think you know something bad has happened." I paused for a moment to see if there was anything she wanted to tell me. I wasn't sure what words to use that this little girl would understand. Would she know what suicide means? So many thoughts and questions swirled in my head in only a few seconds. I decided she would understand the word "accident," so I began.

"Tanya, a terrible accident happened and your daddy died ..."

I didn't have to wait long to know whether she could comprehend my message because the look of wonder faded and a look of horror took its place.

I knelt before her as she screamed, "Oh no! Oh no! Oh Daddy. Oh Daddy. Please come back to me. Oh please Daddy! Please come back to me!"

I listened in sorrow as Tanya grieved the loss of her daddy. And there was no one who could make it stop hurting. And yet ...

From way back in the darkness of the farthest room in the neighbor's house I sensed him coming. Through the bedroom, past the kitchen, into the living room came Tanya's uncle—the black sheep of the family—barefoot, tattooed, long-haired, and generally drunk. Without saying a word this red-eyed grief-stricken man gently picked up Tanya, held her in his arms, and they cried together. Their tears mingled into a single river that fell to the scruffy carpet. Indeed, Tanya and her uncle were now a community of broken souls, and I felt privileged to be there while one "of the least of these, my brethren" (Matt. 25:40) cared for another "least of" God's children.

Sometimes chaplains simply watch in awe as the Incarnation comes to life.

THE MOURNING MIST

Chaplains are not the only ones who bring hope and comfort and a faithful presence to those critically injured. So do paramedics and firefighters who have the responsibility of bringing care to the desperately wounded as they offer CPR and administer medication, and make medical assessments. In truth, this cooperative effort is frontline crisis pastoral care by both lay and ordained alike.

***

The crisp night air was rancid with diesel fuel which hung over the highway like a fog. My eyes burned from the fumes and invisible vapors made my lungs ache. It hurt to be there.

Strange objects littered the roadside for fifty yards in all directions. Jagged hunks of hot engine parts slowly cooled and steam rose in the moist air.

To my left, the giant eighteen-wheeler lay on its side in the ditch, its left-front wheel chewed away. Off to my right was the real sorrow. Beyond the remnant of the crumpled car, lay the wounded. Paramedics ringed the still body of a victim. Some watched, some held lights, two gave CPR. I listened to the count as a paramedic depressed the sternum in the desperate hope that the secret of life would return.

I wondered who this victim was. Who loved her? I imagined that she must hunger to be held by those special people, but instead she was in the company of strangers who were doing their best to give her a chance to live again. And those strangers were feeling that their best efforts might fall just short. It hurts to see another so dreadfully mangled, and although I stayed near, I turned aside.

The paramedics who attended to her had no luxury to look away. I watched these people who helped and wondered how they could touch so gently those who were torn to shreds? Like me, they certainly heard the other victim as he writhed in helpless agony. "Am I going to die? Oh help me!" His desperate pleadings would probably stay locked in their souls as well, because we all wanted to offer hope in a moment when there seemed no certainty at all.

To walk hand in hand with such fear and injury day after day and night after night takes a courage greater than most others ever know. These heroic people do their work amid screams of anguish, the rancid smell of charred flesh and diesel fuel, the risk of other vehicles filled with gawkers who ignore the disaster and plow right on. They accept the responsibility of making life and death decisions without the comfort of sterile sheets, antiseptic treatment rooms, or pleasant conditions. Yet their work is often taken for granted and goes unrecognized.

On this crisp winter night, a zillion stars watch from overhead this hundred yards of terror which cradles such sorrow and such courage. We were there. And in the anguish of that event, so hidden yet so real, was the presence of God, who wept.

The Chaplain's Notebook
Part II: A Consideration of Values

Besides the tasks that need to be done, there are a number of values that undergird emergency care, as well.

1. It is the chaplain's task to represent the church in times of crisis at the setting where agony is acute. In a very real sense, when chaplains are working on scene, so is the church also there.

2. The chaplain's willingness to fully enter the moment is a way to make a viable pastoral assessment of how to intervene most meaningfully. If there are obvious and urgent physical needs, so are there needs of value, meaning, and faith that ought to be addressed. Crisis care is a team effort. Chaplains must do the necessary networking and connecting long before an event occurs so that their place on the team is secure and accepted.

3. Experience indicates that a pastoral presence on the scene shows support to the emergency services staff. They know the chaplain is willing to experience the trauma of putting him- or herself on the line with them and become one of them, and the chaplain's credibility goes up. Emergency services workers are loathe to share with outsiders and unless one enters their world, accepts a measure of the risks, knows the same moments, then the chaplain is inevitably an outsider who is rarely fully accepted

4. First-hand presence allows the chaplain to better sense which workers need help. In a crisis, things happen quickly and one must be able to draw upon trust, reliability, and familiarity already established. If a chaplain is already a part of the team, pastoral care is expedited.

5. While there are tasks that sometimes are done, more often than not, the ministry is one of listening, presence, and availability. It is also a willingness to help those involved find meaning in such moments. And it is an opportunity to see the presence of God in moments where God may seem absent.

6. Police chaplaincy work in crisis moments is not intended to undermine the work of any local religious leader or faith community. Chaplains enter these moments to make certain that the healing and hope of faith is present. Whenever possible, the local religious leader ought to be brought into the event as soon as is reasonable. When no such person exists, then the police chaplain may likely accept a wider range of professional tasks such as funerals, or follow-up grief work.

7. The task in crisis ministry is that of providing pastoral care in moments of crisis to all involved: the victim, their loved ones, the offenders, and those caregivers who provide the emergent care.

V

THE RISKS OF
LAW ENFORCEMENT

Law enforcement is risky business. It's just a part of the job, and one either learns to accept it or get out of the work. Even if most of the time a cop's job is monotonously dull, the potential for chaos is but the next call away. Whenever trauma or serious interpersonal conflict happens, it inevitably involves law enforcement personnel.

Though it is not wise to glorify the risks involved, it is just as foolish to ignore them. Any chaplain who would carve out an authentic ministry in police work must be attentive to the risk factors and be willing to accept that some will come his or her way, too.

One need not look for trouble, that is, reach for foolish and heroic possibilities, yet if one does the job correctly, the nature of pastoral care work itself will likely include some measure of risk. To try to avoid risks is to choose to maintain a detached ministry and only be available when the smoke clears. Likely as not, such a style will not really build much confidence with duty officers and they will usually distrust such chaplains.

Some of the most meaningful pastoral care experiences develop in the dead center of a crisis. Chaplains who earn the right to be present, in the field, when the crisis is unfolding are in a position to offer especially effective care. Care offered later by one who was not there has its place; but care offered in the moment has no equal.

As we've discussed in previous chapters, being on scene does not mean that the chaplain has the same responsibilities or authority as do sworn officers of the law. Clearly, there are pastoral gifts to offer, and there are law enforcement tasks to do, and they are not the same. Chaplains must know the difference and know their place.

On September 11, 2001, I watched on television in stunned disbelief as first one then the other World Trade Center towers collapsed into a pile of rubble. The thought of thousands of innocent people being crushed to death in this act of terrorism was overwhelming. I was profoundly saddened and angered. Within a few weeks I left the security of my hospital chaplaincy in Kansas to temporarily work at Ground Zero, offering pastoral care to the rescue workers. A television awareness was powerful, but the reality of being on scene was staggering. I could not go anywhere without wearing a hard hat for safety reasons. While on duty I was required to wear a mask to help keep out the air-borne filth that threatened everyone's health. Early on, the anxiety about other potential threats was the constant backdrop to every day's work.

Risks come in all manner of ways. There are high speed chases, drug raids and domestic violence episodes. There are building searches and exposure to accidents and injuries. People being arrested sometimes want to fight. Chaplains who prove their worth and are allowed to be a part of the team hear the same wails of anguish and see the same destruction of life and limb as do sworn officers, and this often results in officers knowing that you were willing to stand alongside them in the difficult moments of crisis care. It is the willingness to accept facing such risks that builds trust with law enforcement. You have credibility because you were there.

"JUST LIKE DAD" – THE RISK OF INDENTIFYING

As he stepped into my office, I thought he looked around cautiously to see if anyone had seen him. Lots of folks do that. Some don't even want to meet at my office because they think people might wonder why they have an appointment with a mental health chaplain.

"Kevin, good to see you. Come on in," I said as I greeted him. He smiled, nodded a pleasant but quiet hello to my secretary, and noticed several of the pastoral interns working at their desks.

Safely in my office and with the door shut, Kevin sat awkwardly in the chair I offered him. Not so long out of high school, he still had the rock-hard face and thick arms of the high school football player he once was. Sporting the then-current burr haircut of some officers, he looked just like a Marine recruit on an enlistment poster. Young and athletic, he presented well.

But no matter who presents themselves in my office, there is generally an awkward moment before they begin to unravel the layers of issues they would address. This is a time when they take a deep breath and really decide if they want to let me know the pain they feel in their heart. I've been there before, myself, and know it's not easy to begin telling your story to someone you barely know. Generally, the safe, social issues are presented first. Then, in increasing poignancy come the more high-risk matters. Always the officers who visit me are alert to how I receive the material. If it seems I am not sensitive to their issues, they shut down and perhaps never really deal with the pain that hurts so badly that they needed to call me in the first place.

"Well," Kevin began, "they said I should see you. It's about last weekend's suicide. You know, the Andrew Johnson thing? I guess you know I made that call."

I didn't, but such a thing didn't matter so I stayed quiet, giving Kevin the space and time he needed to continue.

"I got the call along with 92 and responded right away. All I heard was that it was a Code Black. I didn't know it was a suicide. Anyway, when I got there, I handled it OK. I mean, it was pretty shitful. You know, he put a .12 gauge to his mouth and blew the back of his head off and it was ugly to see. Still, I handled it OK. But Jesus, Tom," said Kevin as his eyes filled with tears, "when I found out he was only forty-nine years old and was depressed because he got laid off from his job because of a heart condition, I just lost it! … Tom, that's just what happened to my dad. Forty-nine years old. He got laid off from his job because he had M.S. and could never work again and he killed himself, too. Oh Jesus, Tom, I could take the visual scene. I mean, it was pitiful to see, but nothing got to me until I learned it was so much like Dad. That's what hurt!"

I looked closely at Kevin, who was so young, strong, and handsome. He shifted the Glock 9 mm automatic he wore on his right side to a more comfortable position. His chest, fullback-thick anyway, looked even more imposing as the black, bulletproof vest added ever so slightly to his bulk. Protected by weapon and vest, he was secure behind his armor. Except, of course, no one is ever so protected that life will not find some tiny opening, and through it learn where one is vulnerable after all. Through these tiny cracks our tears will escape, even when we try to keep them hidden.

Kevin went on: "Oh God, I remember that Saturday. Mom asked me to call my dad for lunch. She had made chili for him to eat while he watched the football game, and I went outside to find him. When I opened the garage door I saw him standing there with his shotgun in his mouth. I screamed, 'No! Dad, No!' But it was too late. I ran as fast as I could towards him, but not fast enough, and I watched as his head blew apart. Oh Jesus, Tom, that's what hurts! That's what hurts! That's what hurts! I had to deal with Dad's suicide all over again!"

And in the silence of my office, Kevin buried his head in his hands and wept.

After a few moments he continued. "I don't want the other guys to think I can't handle my job and I don't want them to feel they can't depend on me. I *do* think I can handle whatever comes, but when I heard how much the Johnson case was like Dad's, well, it was just too close." Indeed it was.

Make no mistake about it: cops *are* as tough as they appear. And yet they are as fragile as the rest of us. As chaplains we need to go as gently with them as we would with anyone we love and care for.

THE RISKS OF A DRUG RAID

Five thirty on a Saturday morning. I was keyed up and ready to go! My own excitement embarrassed me, but I had to own it. Perhaps it was even good. You need some excitement for a drug raid. The risk is too high for it to be simply "business as usual." When I arrived at the sheriff's office, I rode down the elevator with 916. Inside the briefing room, I made my way to the coffee and doughnuts for a quick breakfast, eavesdropping on the casual conversation of the other officers all assembled for the raid. Forty-six of them! Representing local city officers, county deputies, highway patrol, plus a canine unit. Also here were neighboring city officers, the KBI and men from the Governor's office. We all mingled, and passed the time telling stories of other raids. In time, the room quieted down and I listened as 904 reviewed each suspect, then outlined the possible risks, and whether there were known weapons in the houses to be raided.

No one said it directly, but here and there references revealed the hidden anxiety that was just underneath the surface. "Got your vest on, don't you?" said one officer. "Yep," the second officer responded. "Don't want another Wichita," said a third—referring to the sad killing of an officer from that nearby city in a recent drug bust. I wondered if that raid had started with just this kind of conversation.

Everyone else here probably thought about Wichita too, but no one spoke directly about it. It's part of the risk. It goes with the job. We wouldn't be here if we didn't know that and accept it. And we all stake our courage on the statistics which reassure us that this is a small town raid, not an urban one, and that the odds are in our favor. (And if we repeat this to ourselves enough, it may make it true.) Even so, a memory like that is one of those realities that is measured by the sweaty palms, the too frequent jokes, and the way veteran officers look at the rookies on their teams. Their eyes betray their question: "Can *he* be counted on if it all falls apart?" I know that's what some on my team wonder about me too. I can't blame them for that.

I also catch myself looking at those young rookies, some not much older than my sons, and I wonder how they feel about such responsibility at such a young age. "I gotta stop thinking that way, though," I tell myself. I don't want to be like an old man who wonders if the new generation has what it takes.

"You want to ride with us, Chaplain?" asked 403, an officer from a nearby community.

"Yeah, thanks," I replied, glad for his invitation.

Once in the area we parked down the street from our suspect's house. Six fifty-five A.M. My own inner tension was betrayed by the dumb jokes I cracked. I hated that about myself, but then again all three of us tried to break the morning tension with forced humor. I found a little relief in the thought that even the veteran cops were anxious.

No matter how experienced they are, it *can't* be "just routine" for these cops. To go to a house before the occupants are up, pound on their door, scream out loudly who you are and what your purpose is! Then to kick in the door and burst in like ambassadors from hell; scramble through every room and secret place with guns drawn; arrest the subjects before they know which end is up, or can resist arrest, or flush the drugs down the toilet. That's just not normal in any sense of the term!

From the patrol unit just ahead, team leader 909 quickly reviewed the plan. "Hesston unit, you take the back door. You two Newton City units are with Hesston. We'll take the front door. You men with the dogs wait till we have the subjects in custody. We'll notify you. Stand by!" Then from the command post came the long awaited order: "All units. It is seven A.M. Your search warrants are now active. Proceed with your mission. Let's roll!" As our patrol car rounded the corner and stopped near the back of our targeted house, I settled inside myself to take stock of what was going on. This event was serious and risky, the culmination of months of work and lots of undercover drug buys and surveillance, but I couldn't ignore the sense of adventure I felt. My excitement crowded out my fear.

Across the side street an old man in green work pants and white tee shirt opened his door and looked out. His face was perplexed. It was 7:00 A.M. on a spring morning when he stepped out for his morning paper, only to see four squad cars and cops with guns drawn running across his neighbor's yard. Like an NYPD drama, only live and in his own neighborhood! He quickly stepped back inside his house to safety, and then peeked through the curtain of his front door.

Two city cops ran by me on their way to our targeted house. I noticed their faces, too. Both young and full of youth's gusto. I swear, if I didn't know better, they could have been two kids playing a game of cops and robbers. For just a moment, I wondered how seriously they were taking this raid. Games can become deadly. I hoped they found the right balance between enthusiasm and caution. Surprisingly, I was not really afraid. Cautious and careful, to be sure, I wondered if I was taking it seriously enough.

As the five of us approached the back porch, I heard 912 scream from the front, "Sheriff's officers! We have search warrants for this house! Open up!"

Then, pounding … and the aluminum storm door gave way to force. More kicking. More pounding. Someone screamed, "We're in!"

I heard the thud of boots on stairs as officers stormed the second floor. From other secret places, others yelled, "All clear here!" My heart raced.

"They're in!" yelled one Hesston officer to all the rest of us and that fact seemed to energize our back door assault. The young city rookie stood back on his left leg and kicked at the back porch storm door with his right. The glass broke, but strangely enough, did not shatter. He kicked again, but the thin wire screen of the storm door refused to give in. In an absurd way, it seemed to be a test of wills: a young cop wanted in and an old storm door wanted to keep him out. "Dammit!" yelled the cop.

In frustration the officer doubled his fist and slammed it into the wire screen in front of the broken glass. It was not my place to tell him to stop, but I hoped he wouldn't slit his hand open in this personal assault. The mesh screen offered some protection to his doubled-up fist which, mercifully, was only scratched.

From inside, we heard muffled sounds. Outside, we faced another barrier now, a solid wooden back door. I wondered what the neighbors were thinking. Do we look as silly as I fear we do? Five cops who couldn't get in! When we finally made entry into the house through a second door, we were greeted with a deep silence. The pounding and yelling of moments ago was over. Everything smelled musty and old. Cautiously, I stood behind the second city cop as we walked from closet to bedroom to living room. He crouched low and held his Glock in front of him, his eyes scanning the darkness. Shades were pulled and the curtains were drawn shut. Even so, the old place was neat and in order. It hardly looked to be a drug house. Old pictures of yesterday sat silently on a dresser. Doilies rested on the back of an overstuffed chair.

Nowhere did I see the disarray I heard about last year when, after *that* raid, stories were told of houses where drug users lived, people whose lives were so chaotic that human waste lay decaying on the floor and cockroaches feasted on the kitchen counters. I was jolted by this clean, old room, like something out of the 1950s.

Still, my palms were sweaty. I dreaded that, at any second, from some dark, unseen corner or hidden closet, the fury of a shotgun would turn this adventure into hell itself.

"Oh damn!" muttered the cop.

"Yeah?" I said, afraid of what he might have found.

"Oh damn!" he said again, then looked at me. "We've just broken into the wrong house! This is a duplex and this is the wrong side!"

"Oh, damn!" is right.

I looked about in astonishment. We'd just kicked in the door to the wrong duplex. No wonder it was so nice!

"Better check around to see that we haven't scared some old woman to death," I tell the cop. "Yeah," he responds, hoping against hope that the place is as deserted as it feels.

Back outside at the right duplex, a deputy has unlocked the first obstinate back door and says with a hint of superiority, "You guys want in here?"

As I step through the open door into the right house and over the jagged pieces of broken glass, the two drug subjects—a male and a female, handcuffed, anxious, in pajamas, and not fully awake, are led down the stairs from their bedroom. They don't look like any of my stereotypes. Once more I face the truth I should have known all along: the two subjects look like normal, decent kids. Like my kids. I'm angry at myself that I let the stereotype of drug users contaminate my own good judgment. Sellers, users, and abusers though they may be, they are still people and imaging them as "pukes" never helps. What they were suspected of doing was certainly illegal and fraught with risks, and they may have been, indeed, as guilty as charged, but still it doesn't help to live by stereotypes.

While another officer handled the legal procedures of the arrest, I did what I always do. I let the event and the moment teach me more about life. In our frenzied haste, we simply got disoriented and kicked in a door which, though unmarked and confusing, was still the wrong door.

A picture on the mantle caught my attention—a high school graduation picture of the arrested girl. She was attractive and wholesome looking. I knew that she had a family who, at this moment, knew nothing of the tribulation that this one they loved so much had tumbled into. I wondered if she had any idea of the searing pain her parents would experience when they faced the truth that their daughter was in serious drug trouble. Would they ever reclaim the hope that filled their lives when she was born nineteen years ago, when all they saw was a life of promise and joy? How quickly life turns. More than likely, she once had promise. She had a future. Now ... ?

On this day, I had pinned on the badge and accepted the commissioned officer's role. It gave me entry into the world of law enforcement. I was on this side of the event today when the doors were kicked in and arrests were made, and I accepted the risks of the raid. Tomorrow I would be working in the hospital, perhaps counseling the parents of a teen-age female dead from an overdose. Not many, except chaplains, walk in and out of such strange worlds and do so by choice.

AT RAINBOW CORNER—IN THE WAY OF GUNFIRE

The early spring evening was cool and my jacket felt good. If the days promised summer, the nights remembered that only a few weeks ago patches of snow still kept to the shadows of trees.

I rode with 915 as we picked our way around the county roads looking for nothing in particular, on an evening of routine back country patrol. Sometimes, we get clear off the black-top and the interstate to dirt roads where it is quiet; where we can stop and watch deer graze along the hedge rows. Four-wheel drive patrol units with steel-studded tires make such patrol possible even in tough weather.

"Nine-fifteen and 909 need you to respond Code 3 to Rainbow Corner. Have the report of shots fired and one subject at or in the gas station itself. K-253, start that way as back-up."

"Nine-fifteen's 10-8."

Nine-fifteen and I raced to the scene, arriving from the east with 909 just seconds behind us as K-253 came from the north.

"See what's inside, Terry," said 915 indicating the gas station, "Ted and I will ask these people what they know." K-253 nodded in agreement. In rural counties where your very life depends on working together, there isn't much of a struggle over who is in control. The various agencies work together as if their lives depend on cooperation, which, in fact, it does.

I followed K-253 inside and watched as a small-framed Hispanic male quickly handed a snub-nosed .38 caliber pistol to the attendant behind the counter, who looked at us in horror as he accepted the revolver from the stranger. Wide-eyed and nervous, the station attendant held the gun at arm's length as if to distance himself from the weapon; he then quickly handed it to me for safekeeping. K-253 turned the suspect around, spread his legs, put his hands on the counter, then patted him down and cuffed him. No more weapons were found.

Shortly, with the suspect seat-belted in the trooper's car, I listened as 915 and 909 filled us in on what sketchy information was known. It wasn't much.

"Apparently this guy and his buddies were working across the highway at Newell's Ranch all week long," said 909. "Looks like they got some beer and were drinking all day. Can't really tell if there's a problem or if they were just shooting for the hell of it. In any case,

Newell said they were running his horses too hard and he told them to quit or he'd fire them. But when he came back, the horses were still wet, the men were drinking, and he told them to leave. He doesn't speak Spanish, so he doesn't know what they said except they all laughed. That pissed him off. He wants them off his land and we're to go help round them up. The men are supposed to be in the barn."

With that, we left the small gas station, crossed Old 81 Highway, and drove down the lane to the parking area between the home, and the boarding house and stables.

Once there, 915 took me aside. "If you're going in, you'll need to carry this." With that, he handed me his extra .12 gauge shotgun. "Remember, when the safety is forward, it's ready to fire. When it's back, it's safe. Stay behind me. Keep your ears open. Be another pair of eyes for me. Look all around and be quiet."

The spring chill seemed suddenly cold. As we walked, our boots made a loud *crunch, crunch* on the top of the crisp mixture of dirt and sand. Silently, 909 turned down the left row of stalls inside the stable, while 915 and I made our way down the right side. I'd never been in a situation like this before. There could be five intoxicated men here, with weapons, who might go crazy and shoot us.

Still, I had to go. I needed to know for myself what it was like to carry a weapon and search a building for unknown subjects, even if only ghosts and quarter horses lived in this stable. I wanted and needed to feel how heavy a .12 gauge shotgun feels when you carry it as an officer of the law, as opposed to carrying it as a hunter. I needed to taste my own anxiety, at close range. This was definitely not TV. The problem with most of us is that we watch too much television. Cops-and-robbers shows abound. But a lot of the time people only get flesh wounds if they are shot at all. Folks want cops to stop crime and violence, and do it all without hurting anyone.

As we moved through the barn the stench of the horse manure made the air thick. The quarter horses looked at us but didn't make a sound. Only the dull clunk of our boots broke the stillness of the night air. Soon, with the barn thoroughly searched and no one found, it was determined that the remaining five had left before we arrived.

The idea of a reserve officer who happens to be a chaplain carrying a weapon is offensive to some. Some would say such a conflict of interest is intolerable, and is to be avoided at all cost. But I suggest that if one chooses to be a police chaplain, the risk is always there—any routine event is ripe for violence. This is inherent in law enforcement work. One can always play it safe and not put themselves in a position where such risks might develop. But this is pastoral care offered by remote control. For the most part, chaplains who make these choices are less likely to be accepted because they aren't there when needed. Another alternative for chaplains is to *always* choose to be there, but decline the opportunity to be armed. For some, this is the only morally responsible way to participate. That stance must be respected.

As for me, I wore two hats: that of the chaplain, and that of the commissioned reserve officer. When performing strictly a pastoral duty, I avoided such a conflict of interest. When we were in imminent danger of harm, the deputy always made sure I was able to defend myself and him, too. In that moment, I was there as whomever I needed to be.

HOSTAGE SITUATION—SEEING A TRAGEDY AT CLOSE RANGE

Six thirty A.M. I've fixed my oatmeal, got the kids' cereal out, and was scanning the sports page to see how Vanderbilt's basketball team did and if they've moved up in the Top 20, when the phone rang.

"Chaplain Shane, this is Davis at the dispatch center. We've got sort of a hostage situation going. Are you available to help?"

A "sort of" hostage situation, I thought to myself. How can that be? "Yeah, I'm available. Give me the details."

Already I knew that "a sort of" hostage situation wasn't all there was, as I hurried as quickly as I could to the nearby town where this bizarre event was happening. "That's about it, Tom," the deputy filled me in on the details, as he met me at my van. "Sombitch just went plumb crazy. Ripped off three shots into the floor and I damn near wet my pants. Don't really know why I didn't just blow him away. Hell, I thought he was gonna shoot *me* next. It all happened so fast. I had my hand on my little snub-nosed .38 back-up in my coat pocket and when I heard them three shots I could feel that impulse to pull my own trigger move from my head, down my neck, right through my shoulder and down my arm 'till it came right to my trigger finger. Damn! I don't know why I stopped. Honest to God, I was a half second from blowing him away. Damn crazy world!"

Still a bit breathless, the deputy went on: "He said he'd talk to you, Tom. I've been in there since 4:00 A.M. and couldn't get no-where. Maybe you can. Said he won't hurt no one but himself. Just wants to kill himself. Said if we tried to stop him, though, he'd take one of us with him. Scared the piss outta me, though, when he fired off those three rounds into the floor."

I opened the door to my van, stepped out and pulled my ski coat tightly about me. Just what on earth had I gotten myself into? The bitter winter wind ripped at my face and stung as I moved from my warm car into the frosty morning. How quickly and com-pletely my life had passed from comfort to chaos in the space of twenty minutes.

The tall, lanky deputy who looked more cowboy than cop, walked with me. His leather-like face showed years of just such crisis moments carved into the lines under his eyes. For just a mo-ment, he turned his back to the north wind's blast, cupped his bare hands, lit a Camel, sucked deeply on it and let the smoke drift from his mouth as he said, "Let's see the sheriff."

From the warmth of his Black and White, the sheriff offered me an option. "It's up to you, Tom, whether you go in. We've got two men in there now with him, and Wayne has been with him off and on all morning. He's not threatening anybody else. Just keeps that revolver cocked and pointed right straight at his head. Every time anybody stands up or moves even a little bit, he makes it clear that if they move at all towards him, he'll blow his head off. And I reck-on that .357 would do the job! Says he's got hollow points, too."

Strange how time seems to stop so you can wander around inside special moments and see what's happening. I guess that doesn't make sense, but it's true. An Arctic cold front which sucked temperatures to below zero and a steady north wind made it feel as if tiny, jagged pellets of ice were peppering my face and hands as I stood there learning the details of this unfolding event. Not thirty yards away in an old farmhouse was a forty-five year old man ... a *drunk* forty-five year old man. And on his coffee table was a legal document—divorce papers—and a letter from his wife saying she's had enough of his abuse and his drinking, and was tired of all the broken promises.

Here and there deputies stood outside with winter parkas adding to the bulk of their bullet proof vests. Every so often someone would stomp his feet as if to see if his toes were still alive! Oh, there were the usual jokes cops typically say: "Let's just gas the place and get it over with," or, "Let the sucker just do it and we'll get hot coffee and come back when he's done."

The sound of the sheriff's voice brought me back to the cold reality of my task: "If you do go in, Tom, I want you to wear this vest. It won't make you a hero if you go without it, and it sure as hell won't save your life if you get shot in the head. If something does happen, get the hell out of there!" Not exactly words of comfort and encouragement but delivered with an honesty that I respected.

It was the truth deeper than truth that was most important, but hardest to know. To grasp the truth, you have to stop listening to the noise of the moment and turn inside yourself. And be still. And hear with your heart, not your ears. But be careful. It's ever so much easier to just listen to the words and the clatter. To hear with your heart is a poet's burden, for it attunes you to the secret sins and sorrows that whisper in the silence.

As we walk to the house, I'm right behind 916 and can almost hear the pounding of both our hearts on our bullet proof vests. Neither of us looked scared, but we knew it was a real man with a real gun inside and that we were walking right into the living room where life and death stare at each other.

And there he was. Not six feet from me was a stranger. A man just my age who sat in a green over-stuffed chair with a large plastic glass full of homemade wine between his legs and with his right hand holding a loaded .357 at his temple. I'd never seen such a thing before. I could hardly believe I let myself enter such a moment.

"Well, come on in. Don't be scared. Hell, I ain't gonna shoot you. Ain't got no beef against you or any of these other cops neither. It's them lawyers and judges who I hate. Them's the sonsa bitches I hate."

My heart pounded and I could not control my eyes. Try as I might, I stared at his right hand and the cocked .357. I didn't want him to shoot himself, and even more I didn't want him to shoot me.

As we looked at each other I flashed on a clear memory: two grieving parents sitting slumped in agony on their son's bed, while a black body bag with his remains was wheeled off. The young man had blown his life away with a bullet through his head. And on that hot summer night I watched in silence as a desperate mother and dad got a pan of water from the kitchen, a bright yellow sponge, and washed the remnants of their precious son's shattered bone, tissue and brains off the wall. "Oh Jesus! I hope the Lord understands about Billy and how troubled he was. And I hope he ain't in hell right now," whispered his father, and then he looked down and said, "This is the worst day of our lives."

The melancholy sound of a Willie Nelson song playing in the background brought me back to the present moment: "Forgiving you is easy, but forgetting seems to take the longest time."

The drunken man in the armchair was stirred by it too. "That sombitch Willie tells the truth. Damn straight, he does! Y'all listen to his words. Ole Willie's tellin' it like it is."

Then he was quiet for a moment and I listened to the absolute silence of a broken heart, a broken dream, a shattered life, and the anguish of alcoholism. "I'll tell it to you right straight out. I ain't got no reason to live no more. My wife left me and she was my life. It's all over for me. I got one more song to listen to and I want you to hear it with me, then I'm gonna blow my damn head off. Don't try to stop me or I swear there'll be hell to pay. Some one of you will fucking die with me. I swear!"

With a load of homemade wine boiling his brain, the grizzly old man stumbled across the room, reached his new stereo and turned the volume to its loudest, as Willie Nelson sang, "You wouldn't cross the street to say good bye."

Deeper than Willie's lament was the nearly silent swish as his right hand put his gun one more time to his temple and louder than the music I could hear the *ka-lick* of the hammer as it was pulled back to a ready position. I felt my soul cry in anguish.

"No! Don't!" 916 and I both screamed at once.

I wanted out of that moment. I'd seen the aftermath of tragedy—the highway carnage, the dead bodies, the ripped and torn remains, the head with the hole in it, the body left for days in the winter snow. But I'd never stood there, as it happened, and that immanent prospect sent shivers up and down my soul. But I couldn't leave. Regardless of what it cost me, what I might see, it was my destiny to be there. Perhaps that's the way it always is in a cop's world. As Willie finished his lament, I watched as the old man tried to find the courage to squeeze the trigger. But in spite of his ominous words, something kept him from doing it. So we simply waited. I was relieved when at last the long hours without sleep and the large amount of homemade wine took their toll and the lonely old "hostage" fell into a drunken sleep, his own problems temporarily taking him off the hook. Even so, in the odd moments when I ride in silence with a deputy on the back country roads and we drive by that old farmhouse, I see myself in all my fears, dread, and even a measure of courage, and know I'm different because of that bitter, winter day once upon a time.

JESUS AND THE VELVET WOMAN – AT RISK FROM AN ANGRY FAMILY

I stepped over the broken end table and waded through the scattered dishes and overturned pots and pans. In the nearby corner of the living room, in the brown fuzzy chair, sat a young woman. Her blue jeans lay rumpled on top of the jumble of magazines and newspapers scattered about the floor. A pink sheet covered her legs below her sweatshirt. She held hands with a friend, a neighbor woman from down the street, who knelt beside her. She shook from head to foot and her eyes were swollen from crying. One wrist was still red from the struggle of a little while ago.

"Miss Smith, this is our chaplain. Maybe it will help to talk to him while we go look for the man." That was my introduction to the woman—a woman who wondered whether to cry in fear or in rage. In truth, both feelings boiled inside her, the understandable result of the terror she had just known when a stranger tried to rape her.

"But he couldn't get the job done," she said in a trembling voice. "He tried, but I fought too hard! I was scared. I kept telling him not to, that it wasn't right, but he kept on trying. That's why this house's a mess. I ripped those drawers clean out trying to find that butcher knife over there. Found it, too. I'd a killed the son of a bitch if I could've. I told him if he came any closer I'd split him right open. Would've too! For damn sure I would've!"

And there it was. Right on the coffee table. The knife. Beside it lay the splintered pieces of a child's model car, an innocent victim of the chaos. For a moment, I allowed myself to soak up a sense of this home. Who was she, and what was her life really like? A few of the woman's friends sat around the couch as if in silent vigil. A little girl, the woman's daughter, hugged a tiny tiger kitten so tightly I wondered if its eyes would pop right out. On the north wall was a gigantic picture of Jesus. Just the head, but with eyes that looked all about the room in such a way that wherever you were, Jesus looked right at you. Jesus saw it all—the weeping woman, the numbed neighbors, the cluttered kitchen, the frightened little girl with her kitten, the cold and still butcher knife, and even me.

Of course this Jesus saw the picture on the south wall, too, A nude woman whose splendor stood in intricate detail for all to see. A picture so crystal clear that no one could help but notice her as she stood so soft and still on black velvet.

Jesus, the velvet woman, the assault victim, the butcher knife, and the chaplain who stood in the center of an unraveling moment trying to catch one thread and tie it solidly. Like some bizarre movie plot, only pathetically real. And hostile, too. This event seemed particularly lethal. The victim's dad had been summoned, by someone, and had come to find justice for his daughter. You could feel his rage more than see it. His deep-set eyes blazed and his thick, tattooed arms strained like cables as he slammed one fist into the other.

"And where was that no-good boyfriend of yours when it happened? He knows there's prowlers and peepin' Toms around here and he's supposed to be here with ya. He never was worth a damn nohow. I'll kill him, too, if he comes back." So yelled the father. He mentioned some old, unsettled score about money the boyfriend borrowed and never paid back; proof enough to the angry dad that the boyfriend was not good enough for his daughter. And now this assault! It was payback time.

And then things got worse. The boyfriend arrived. In a burst of fury, the doors to the mobile home burst open and he entered the small living room, his own rage ready to blow. Someone had already told him. And he was ready to rip, and claw, and pound for his girlfriend's honor. Or something.

"Who the hell are you?" he screamed at me.

But I was one step ahead. Already I had my badge in my sweating left hand. "I'm Chaplain Shane, Newton Police Department." Thank heavens he accepted the silver star and paid me no more attention.

In the next moment he saw the dad, and he's furious at him for being drunk and never taking care of the family. The two angry men stare at each other like two male animals. For just a second, all of life holds its breath. I tried to be reasonable. It seemed to be a necessary but crazy thing to be. "Why don't you two let things cool down?" I said. "Whatever your problems are, take care of them later. Right now, Michelle needs all the support she can get. Your fighting won't help"

What do chaplains do? It's hard to say. Sometimes we listen to a weeping woman who sits in helpless rage because a stranger has attempted to violate her. Sometimes we try to bring good judgment and order into the center of confusion. Sometimes we try to get next to seething rage and hope that it doesn't blow up and hurt us too. And sometimes we can't help but smile at the absurd humor of watching such a drama take place between Jesus and the velvet woman who hang so silently on two opposing walls and watch each other.

MATT SAMUELS—WHEN DEATH STRIKES A PARTNER

The drive from Newton to Eureka skirts the edge of the Flint Hills and looks as much like the open range of the Wild West as any place does. The gentle hills stretch to the horizon. Hawks soar lazily overhead, catching a ride on the ever-present prairie wind as they scan for food.

Sometimes I fantasize about leaving the highway and finding a trail through the open range to explore what lies beyond each rolling hill. I love my work, both as a hospital chaplain and as a police chaplain, but it is work that confronts my nearly every day with suffering. The prairie invites me to slow down, to listen, to set aside the sorrow of my work and be quiet. The prairie has no enchanting forests to linger in, no mountains that tower above the clouds, and no craggy coast lines with waves crashing endlessly over rocks. The prairie, at least what's left of it, is open range. It's a place where you can watch the sun rise and set with an unencumbered view and feel a gentle peace that soothes your soul. This trip to Eureka was different. I kept hearing Sheriff Motter's voice in my mind as the solitary miles slipped by.

"Do you know what's going on?" he had asked.

"No, I've been too busy at the hospital to take notice of any news."

Motter was quiet on the other end. His normal upbeat demeanor was gone. "Matt Samuels, the Greenwood County Sheriff, was killed this morning while serving a warrant."

Sheriff Motter was thirty miles away, but I could picture him in his office. As he told me this awful news his voice cracked with emotion. Sheriffs in Kansas know one another. The news was sketchy, but troublesome. Responding to a tip that a wanted subject was at a house in a lonely section of the county—someone wanted for parole violation and staying in a possible meth lab house—Matt Samuels and two deputies went to apprehend the man.

Things are sometimes very different in the country, where offenders and deputies can know one another. Sometimes the best tactic for law enforcement is a low-key, informal, face-to-face encounter rather than a show of force. It lowers the intensity level. But that didn't work on this day. Without warning, when Samuels entered the door and started up a flight of stairs, shots were fired. He was struck and tumbled to the ground, fatally wounded. The deputies with him provided what care they could, but were pinned down by the assailant's gunfire even as they tried to administer CPR.

"Are you able to go to Eureka and offer support to them?" asked Sheriff Motter. "They've asked our Critical Incident Stress Management Team for help." Within minutes I was underway.

Eureka, Kansas is a sleepy little community, a county seat and home to maybe 2500 people. My wife's grandmother lived there, and here we first experienced her Alzheimer's disease when she didn't know us on a visit. It's a town that I associate with sorrow. But it is also a town where my church has a camp and where I have spent a few nights in quiet solitude refreshing my spirit. Eureka is like any town, anywhere. But on this day, it was a town filled with anger and sadness.

Sheriff Matt Samuels was a third generation law enforcement officer in Greenwood County, Kansas. His dad had been sheriff there before him. Well loved and respected, Matt had the knack of upholding the law in a way that you felt obligated to pay attention to him. He worked *with* his people, not just for them. That is why he was greeted with a smile and a wave throughout the county.

When he got a tip on the morning of January 19, 2005 that Scott Cheevers, who was wanted for various legal offenses, was at a house in Hilltop—a forlorn settlement of a few homes twenty-some miles northeast of Eureka—he and a couple of deputies went there to serve the warrant.

At one time, Cheevers appeared to be a promising child in spite of a troubled home life. He was a kid with athletic ability and took third at the state track meet in the long jump. But he made a wrong turn, one that took him deeper into the world of drugs, with methamphetamines. After that, he seemed completely lost. Cheevers did time in prison and even got into trouble there for using drugs, and for other offenses. Eventually he got out, but he couldn't seem to shake that lifestyle and, like a magnet, he drew drug users and other malcontents. He always had a choice, yet he always seemed to choose wrongly.

Since Cheevers had ignored the requirement to stay in contact with his parole officer, a warrant was issued for his arrest. It should have been a routine pick-up. Of all the sheriffs he might have had to face, Matt Samuels—who had as much compassion as legalism—was the one coming to serve the warrant. Matt's mom, in fact, was a third cousin to the sheriff, so there was at least the hope that family ties would have given him a fair hearing.

Outside the sheriff's office at the back of the City Hall, a dozen officers from a half-dozen tiny nearby towns milled about talking softly to one another. Some smoked. Others stood by themselves, peering into space as if searching for answers. Nearby, two TV trucks from Wichita with their antennae jacked high waited to report the unfolding events as bits of news came to light. As a stranger to this community, I could feel the guardedness that comes to groups and individuals when they feel besieged. Walls go up. Strangers are viewed with suspicion. People close ranks. But when your department is rocked by tragedy, of necessity you accept help from other agencies. An event this staggering shows that the law enforcement community is as tightly-woven as a blanket.

"I'm Chaplain Shane from the Harvey County CISM team. I've been asked to check in with the undersheriff. Can you tell me where to find him?"

Then, a familiar face. A KBI agent I've worked with on other occasions offered a warm greeting. Just the blessing I needed to be seen as acceptable.

"I think the undersheriff is inside," the friendly agent said. "Just ask for him and tell him who you are."

The small department was filled with people and cigarette smoke. In a tiny room, off the main squad room, a dispatcher sat at the console taking calls, most of them from well-wishers calling in to express their sorrow. In a larger room, a middle-aged woman named Sharon was at her desk. Every small-town department has a "Sharon." She was a civilian who was the department "mother," and her care and support were the glue that held people together. Sharon knew everything—who had been on scene and what had happened; which dispatchers fielded the calls, and who worked in spite of and beyond their own horror; which ones were hiding behind their macho masks, and which ones were barely holding on. She also knew which officer did CPR on the sheriff and which ones were fired on.

The undersheriff was still on the scene, Sharon told me, but she had known that I was coming and was glad I was there.

Six hours had passed since the shooting. The initial shock had worn off, and the full weight of the tragedy was being felt. A profound sadness smothered the rooms of the department. Looks of grief gave way to anger, but there was nothing to do but stand in small groups and watch the news. The Kansas State Trooper SWAT team was still on scene with the alleged perpetrator barricaded in the house, occasionally firing at them.

While I waited for the rest of my CISM (Critical Incident Stress Management) team to arrive, I listened to as many stories and made as many connections as I could with the officers who were willing to talk.

Sharon let me know that those most impacted were the deputies who were with the fallen sheriff, plus two dispatchers who took the initial call and who sent out requests for back-up to other deputies, and to state troopers from neighboring towns who listened to the drama from all around the county. Six hours earlier, those same dispatchers had summoned the paramedics to the scene for a Code 3 hot call run to the Hilltop home. Then they had listened to the tension of the officers making the call who reported, "Officer down! Officer shot!" Miles away in a closed office, they had to wait while time crawled by and help hurried to the scene. In spite of their expediting the calls, follow-through all seemed fatally slow. These same dispatchers had been the link between the deputies pinned down trying to do CPR, even as they attempted to drag the wounded sheriff to safety; the same deputies who were fired on from somewhere deep inside the house.

Sharon correctly assessed that our first intervention ought to be with the on-scene deputies and the dispatchers. Preparing myself for the work ahead, I wondered what it was like to watch as your sheriff was gunned down, then try to do CPR in the middle of gunfire. What an example of extraordinary courage under the most difficult of circumstances!

Characteristic of most traumas, the day was marked by moments of intense action followed by the hard job of waiting. So I waited while the deputies who had gone home were called back, and I listened to the stories of anyone who would talk, witnessing to emotions from horror, to rage, to sorrow.

A beloved sheriff had been shot to death in cold blood, a classic example of doing everything the right way, yet losing the battle. It was a sad demonstration of the high risk of law enforcement, and how the worst consequences can erupt in what could be seen as a routine call. The truth was obvious—there are no routine calls. And, ordinary officers can and do rise to heroic stature in times of crisis.

The resulting anger was raw and evident, always managed and never unleashed. But I felt it. I saw it in the faces of the officers. I heard it in their curt responses to questions. And I felt it myself. Underneath the professionalism and deeper than the training that drills into officers the right procedures, a brotherhood binds us all together. When one officer is shot, every officer and every department feels it. When one goes down, all of us stumble. Political and personal tensions, and differences that occasionally divided us, melted into insignificance, and the brotherhood closed rank and stood together.

Dusk slowly settled over Greenwood County. Quietly, I walked with the CISM team across the parking lot with the TV trucks still waiting for morsels of news to feed the hungry and interested public, and into the courthouse for our debriefing

We knew that some intervention was appropriate. These five people carried their own emotional and spiritual turmoil from this horrible event, and they deserved our care. This visit would provide basic care, but more care would likely be in order in the days to come.

Several days later, at the funeral, Sheriff Motter gave me a black band to cover my badge—one way in which we honored an officer killed in the line of duty. Deputies came from all across Kansas. State Troopers by the dozen arrived to manage the traffic and funeral procession. City police officers from around the state; fish and game representatives; the KBI. Somewhere in the several thousand mourners, the Governor was in attendance as were other elected state officials and a U.S. Representative. It was more than a political show, it was a genuine expression of grief and support—for the slain sheriff's family, the Greenwood County Sheriff's Department and, quite frankly, for all of law enforcement. One officer was murdered and every officer was impacted.

A brisk wind howled across the prairie. Half-mast flags flew in the breeze in full form as if even nature wanted to do its part to make sure this day was acknowledged.

The gym where the ceremony was to take place was full. So was the auditorium where Butler County Community College had set up a closed circuit TV to cover it. Even the hallways were full, as hundreds of officers, myself included, stood unable to find any place inside to hear or witness the funeral.

In a way, it didn't matter. It was enough to be there. It was enough to make the effort to show support. It was enough for me to be present with the deputies with whom I have worked for nearly thirty years. Such rituals do not alter the facts nor do they take away the oppressive grief felt by the victim's loved ones. But they do show solidarity and support and it is the right thing to do.

Matt Samuels left a legacy that will live for as long as there are decent citizens who value law and order and justice. It can be said of him: "Well done, good and faithful servant. Well done." (Matt. 25:21)

Scott Cheevers was ultimately apprehended and charged with one count of capital murder, three counts of attempted murder, one count of criminal possession of a firearm, and several drug related violations.

KURT FORD—THE RISK OF HEARTBREAK

"Chaplain Shane?" asked the stranger.

"Yes," I answered. I shook the sleep out of my mind and tried to make out the voice. I didn't know her. Nighttime calls almost always mean tragedy. Somewhere, something awful had happened. I just didn't know what. I knew it wasn't Newton Dispatch on the phone because they always identify themselves, but someone had a serious concern. That was obvious in her voice. It was 3:30 in the morning. I sat on the edge of the bed waiting.

"Chaplain Shane, this is Martha Jenkins. I'm a nurse at Newton Medical Center. We need you to come to the Emergency Department." She paused for a moment as if what she had to say next was harder than she expected. "We've had a deputy killed."

"Oh my God," I thought. Instantly, sleep vanished and without any intentionality on my part, my body was alert. In the silence that followed the nurse's announcement, my mind raced with possibilities. Who works nights now? Maybe there was a chase and a car wreck. But already I sensed that this tragedy would be personal. This was my department and these were my friends. One of them was dead. I dreaded to know who.

"Can you say who? And what happened?" I had to know.

"It was Kurt Ford. He was shot."

"Oh my God," I thought again. Shot! I swallowed my horror and tried to focus. I needed more data. "How did it happen?"

"There was a hostage situation and he was killed. Can you come?"

"Yes, of course."

Kurt Ford. I knew him well. Everybody knew him well because he never knew a stranger. He was one of those deputies who was universally liked. Because he graduated from high school with my older daughter, I had known him for years. From the start, our age difference was never an issue. We related deputy to chaplain. Man to man. Friend to friend. A huge lump in my throat formed and would not go away. I blinked back my tears. I had to put all of that on hold. There would be time for my grief later on. Now was the time to find my way through all the broken dreams and broken hearts I would meet.

I had worked for thirty years as the sheriff's chaplain and I'd delivered countless death messages. I'd ridden in the right front seat for thousands of miles. I'd listened to stories of marriages that had turned to dust and kids who had made wretched choices. I'd married deputies and buried their loved ones. I listened to a deputy once choke back his tears as he told me that his brother was charged with first degree murder. I'd been in chases and drug raids. I'd broken up fights. But I'd never before done a line of duty death. In that instant, every sad moment I'd ever worked came back to haunt me. And it was only the beginning.

Small town, Newton, America. The second smallest county in the state. We have our share of murders and drug problems and lots of burglaries of farm homes. Sometimes we have to work a homicide. Mostly it is a lot of road time running radar and checking doors late at night, never a line of duty death! This kind of tragedy happens somewhere else.

Only two months ago Sheriff Matt Samuels was killed, and now after thirty years as a law enforcement chaplain I had my second line of duty death in two months.

Kurt was dead. I rode with him two Saturdays ago. We talked at length about his hopes to one day be sheriff. He would have been a good one, too.

More than almost any other pastoral event, I was torn between my own feelings of sorrow and anger and my professional responsibilities to care for the officers with whom I work. For the moment, I compartmentalized my feelings. My priority was care for the deputies and Kurt's family. This tragedy would devastate them. He left a wife and two sons. The thought of telling them was oppressively sad.

The door to the ambulance entrance was open when I arrived at the hospital. The paramedics clustered together looking both sad and stunned. They nodded their greeting, but respected my obvious mission. They were emotionally wounded, too. Just outside the trauma bay, Sheriff Motter put his phone away, grabbed me in a big bear hug and wept. "He's dead, Tom! He's dead. He was like my son!" In this mournful cry of grief the usual façade of law enforcement toughness was overwhelmed by human compassion.

Cops *are* tough. They have to be. More than most people they work with all manner of suffering and sorrow. They work with offenders who inflict horrible suffering on their victims. They work with victims whose lives are forever changed because of someone else's callous disregard for the lives of others. Being tough lets you place a barrier between yourself and this world of sorrow. But some tragedies are too profound and there is no place to hide. It's best if you have a person and a place to unburden your soul. This is the hidden side of law enforcement that most never see. But I do. Every chaplain does. I work in a hospital, in a level 1 trauma center. Every day, strangers are brought to our facility in a crisis. Some die. Some never walk again. Some will leave but with radical, life changing consequences. Some are healed. But almost always they are strangers to me. It seems easier that way. I don't know their stories or their dreams. I don't know about their families. I don't see them long after the tragedy or understand all the ways their lives have changed. Tonight it was personal.

"He's in here, Tom," said the sheriff as he pulled back the curtain around the gurney, and we stood silently by Kurt's side. I blinked back my tears and swallowed hard ... or I tried to. I felt more feelings than I could sort out. I was mostly sad, but I was also angry. It didn't have to happen! The perpetrator chose violence over reason. How dare he?

It was quiet in the trauma room. Kurt and I were now separated by the barrier that stands between the living and the dead. I felt some of the sorrow and anger I felt while working at Ground Zero in New York City. Thousands of good people died needlessly and senselessly and I was impacted by the work. But they too were strangers. Tonight the senseless act involved someone I knew. Outside the trauma room, Max, the retired undersheriff, stood quietly. I have no better law enforcement friend than Max. He had agreed to stand vigil with Kurt so he would not be alone and so the other deputies could carry out their work. I saw it as a gift of honor to a fallen brother.

I rode with Sheriff Motter through the nighttime streets of Newton to Kurt's home. It had to be done. And it had to be done soon. This kind of news takes on a life of its own and like a prairie fire it scorches the earth wherever the wind blows it. In only a matter of time word would leak out and someone would call the family to offer condolences or see if it were true.

The sheriff's spotlight illuminated the street number in the front of Kurt's home. We parked in front and walked up the steps onto the porch. The night was damp and cold.

"You're going to have to tell her, Tom," said the sheriff. "I can't do it." Long ago I made my peace with this responsibility. Sometimes cops *have* to deliver bad news but most prefer to have it done by a chaplain. It's what we do. I've done it more times than I can remember in three decades, but it is never a memorized script and it is never easy. There are times when I am haunted by old memories of especially difficult notifications. This notification would be one that would never leave me. I carry it in my heart forever.

The sheriff rang the doorbell and the dogs barked to alert the family. I could see Kurt's wife peek through the curtain to see who it was that so rudely awakened her at 4 A.M. I can only imagine what she felt. That it was the sheriff and me was some comfort, but she must have known that we were there because something was dreadfully wrong.

She looked at us with sleep draining away, replaced by an on-rush of dread. She tried so hard to be composed. "What's wrong?" she asked.

Only a few hours ago, when Kurt received a call activating the Emergency Response Team, he had suited up and left. She said goodbye. A familiar routine. Wives of ERT members more or less make their peace with it. The dread never goes away entirely, but you come to terms with it.

She looked at us, waiting our response to her question. I was glad for the darkness. I hoped it gave me enough shadows to center myself and find the courage to tell her this awful truth. In this sacred moment, I knew a truth that would forever change her family. I knew a truth that would bring great sorrow to them. I have chosen this ministry and believe it to be my calling. But it is a sacred trust that comes with a cost. She looked at me as I spoke.

"We need to tell you that there has been an incident with the Emergency Response Team. Kurt was shot. He was taken to the hospital where he died."

I tried to be sensitive. I tried to be compassionate. I tried to tell the truth with a simple, direct, understandable honesty. But no matter how I tried and no matter what I said, I knew it hurt.

It was quiet in the living room. She sat on a footstool trying to take in the meaning of the message. There isn't room enough in one's heart to make a place for this new reality. One horrific tragedy and one sobering message have changed everything.

VI
SUICIDE AND PASTORAL CARE

The deputy and I left West Lake Park where we had just awakened a family in a camper to tell them of a relative's death in an out-of-county car wreck. Our mood was one of thoughtful reflection. It's often that way. After telling a family that someone they love is suddenly dead, it prompts those of us who break the news to reflect on the nature of life. Life is such an ever-present reality that most of us never detach ourselves enough to think about it. We accept it without question.

On this night, the deputy was quiet for awhile then opened his concerns to me. "You know, Tom, I can accept death. I mean, I can accept how some people are so old or so sick or so injured in a car wreck that they just let go. I know there are some times when the illness is so bad and there is no known cure, or they are a Code Blue at the scene that they just plain give up. But what I can't understand is how a person could actually decide to take their own life. To kill themselves. I don't think I've ever been at the point where I couldn't see some possibility. Some chance. I just don't understand how a person can't see hope."

Of all matters in crises ministry, suicide may well be the most difficult to understand. The deputy was correct, from his own perspective. He couldn't imagine how someone could *decide* to kill himself because he had never stood in that most dreadful of all places—that lonely point of despair where absolutely no hope is to be found. So long as a flicker of possibility remains, we can hang on. Most of us find that little piece of hope and, though battered and nearly crushed in spirit, we cling by our fingertips to life because somehow, some way, we sense it can get better, and usually it does.

Many of us *have* been so broken in spirit that, for just a frightening moment in time, we actually gave a serious thought to suicide.

Maybe we were in such emotional pain that we were ready to give up, hoping that some bizarre accident or illness would claim us and we wouldn't have to do it ourselves. Then again, if we are in enough despair, we may have entertained the idea of our own pro-active choice to kill ourselves. Maybe we even took the .38 from the old shoe box, all wrapped up in an old towel and safely hidden away in the top of the closet, and drove to some far-off county road. Perhaps we felt the weight of the little snub-nosed weapon as it pressed against our temple. Maybe for a split second we stood at the brink, yet decided there was some possibility for life, however remote it was.

If you have ever looked into this bleak moment in your own life, you may be able to stand more compassionately beside the rest of your sisters and brothers who have gotten lost in this horrid place.

A dear friend of mine knew such despair after his divorce. But, like so many of us, he swallowed his agony and went on like the good soldier he was. The agony turned to anguish and he tumbled deeper into hopelessness. Needing to fill the empty evening hours, he got a second job tending bar and doubling as a bouncer. When a familiar ex-con known to carry a knife became disruptive one night, he had to throw him out. Grabbing the man by both arms my friend did so, knowing that the drunk would either go willingly or turn on him and perhaps try to injure or kill him.

"It didn't matter to me either way," he said. "If it worked my way, then maybe I found the lost courage and hope I couldn't seem to find. If he killed me, then that was just as OK. I couldn't live much longer in as much pain as I was feeling. It had to get better or I had to die." My friend's was a passive suicide ideation. Unwilling to take the initiative himself, he was willing to put himself in a position where it might happen to him.

At its heart, suicide is a theological condition because it develops where hope is absent. Like cancer, this despair takes on a life of its own and eats up even healthy possibilities. What makes this kind of despair so evil is that, often as not, it is based on a *perceived* reality as much as any *objective* reality. If one perceives there is no hope, then for all practical purposes there isn't any. To another, hope is seen as possible; to the despairing one, it is not even a dream.

Bridging that seemingly endless chasm from perceived to objective reality is very difficult. Herein lies the chaplains task—to help people in overwhelming despair come to new hope and to see reality from a completely different vantage point.

There is no point in being naïve about life, however. If hope is only seen in the absolute resolution of a problem or a complete restoration of health, relationships, or some previous condition, there is no hope. One must redefine hope to be less a "cure" and more a "healing." One must acknowledge that some relationships are, in fact, irreparably destroyed. But possibilities for a new type of relationship ... a new view on life ... may still exist nevertheless.

Some new vision of hope is possible. It's not an easy shift, however. It requires a difficult letting go of precious old visions and a willingness to set them aside in favor of something new. Those old dreams once seemed to promise life and joy. The thought of giving them up and reaching for some cold new possibility asks for more than seems fair.

If suicide is a theological condition resulting from the loss of hope, then it is just as true that the faith community has a difficult time responding to this issue because of its own prejudices. Some in the church are too quick to judge. Some are unable to see the human struggle in this issue and categorize the whole episode as one of sin. Such a point of view offers little comfort to anyone involved in this dilemma, whether victim or survivor.

Within the ministerial community, it may be a lot easier for some to keep a safe distance from despairing people than it is to fully encounter the pain of someone who is suicidal. After all, by definition, a pastoral encounter calls for one to stand so close to the wounded other that their tears may wash off onto your own cheeks if you truly embrace that hurting one. Who wants to stand that close to despair and embrace it? You might get touched by it yourself.

Judgment and condemnation for a decision made from a position of despair is hardly a redemptive pastoral act. The offering of healing and hope seem a far more blessed response.

THE DEAD END STREET

A block off Main Street, just a few hundred yards from everyday folks doing everyday things, the street dead ends and doesn't go anywhere. As I walk it, come along. If you are a cop, however, you may have to give up the usual self-control and raw courage that seems embedded in you. But, I assure you that no one will see if just this one time you leave the badge on the shelf, put the 9mm in the locker, and join us as the ordinary person you really are.

"Ambulance one gives one Signal 4 [suicide], Code Black [dead]. Call the coroner." A crisp, no-nonsense message.

"Eight-eight, you want me to call the chaplain, too?" asks the dispatcher to the beat officer on the scene. "Ten-four. Subject's one-half [wife] was here but didn't come in. We got more family to tell. Have 606 meet me here."

A Signal 4 … If you look at the moment from far enough away, it is just another piece of work. Just a suicide. And who wants to see it for what it *really is*—a moment of broken dreams when family members hurt, and hurt, and hurt, until it seems there will never be hope or healing again.

Just a block off Main Street. Just a few hundred yards from Sunday evening churchgoers and teenagers cruising. Not so far, really, from my home—where the sounds of my family are heard even as I step up into my Dodge van. I looked through the half-opened curtains at the people I love before I left to embrace a moment of sorrow. Sara was playing with our cat, Molly. Mike and Mark wondered about "That Signal 4, that Black Signal 4." Our older daughter Kim was making a last-minute call to a friend before she went back to college. And my wife Linda watched me with sad eyes, knowing I'd come home affected by the horrible event that had happened.

My police radio continued with the normal evening communication. I'm on my way to a house of trauma and the radio traffic talks about an opossum in a yard and even a notice to "check the area behind First United Methodist Church. Apparently, three juveniles were spotted climbing a tree!" When I arrived at the scene I realized that I'd been at this house before, about six months ago, when another person took his life. First it was a retired cop, and tonight it was a business man. Both died in the same house. It must not be a home at all, just a place down at the end of Lonely Street where people go to die.

I walked up the concrete steps and knocked on the door. Eight-eight answered, telling me to come in. "Hello, Chaplain. You're here before the coroner arrives. Last Saturday when that guy tried to 'off' himself at the jail, you were there before the ambulance, and here you are again!" No matter what the occasion, cops will find something to joke about.

I take his bizarre greeting and answer in kind. "Well, you know me, 88. I just can't stay away. Guess I have a nose for these sorts of things. What've we got?"

"He's there in the kitchen on the floor. Took an overdose. Left a note on the coffee table. Guess the loss of his job and his divorce was just too much. It's kinda sad. His name's John Krehbiel. You know him?"

There's not another sound in the entire house as I stand alone in the kitchen with unknown John Krehbiel. I bend down close and peek into those empty eyes. He would never hear the crying of his own little boys, his ex-wife, his parents, or his sisters. He could never understand how horribly he had hurt those he tried so much to love.

It hurts to be here. He was a man just like us until a few hours ago when he got lost in life and found a quick way out. I wondered how God understands such moments. And where do broken families find even a grain of hope so that they can glue themselves back together and go on?

I wandered by myself through the empty rooms of the house and listened for echoes from the past. I looked around his bedroom.

The bed was neatly made. A bottle of aftershave sat on the dresser and a notebook of his writing was beside it. A bulletin board held nearly a hundred photographs of days gone by. In one he was smiling as he held a baby. Once upon a time life must have seemed filled with promises, and love, and intimacy. You could see it in his grin as he looked at the baby, a so-big man and a so-little baby together in a bond of incredible closeness. There was a time when he could hear the birds singing, when he could smell the flowers, and when there was pleasure to give and receive.

Back in the kitchen, so still on the floor, was the bitter truth that dreams do die. "All the king's horses and all the king's men …"

"What do you think, 606? Kinda spooky, huh? You know whose place this was, don't you?"

Ninety-three was speaking to me. He was standing in the hallway outside the bedroom and caught me by surprise as I looked at the bulletin board.

"Yeah, I do. It was Mack, the retired cop's place. You worked that one too, didn't you?" I replied.

"I did. This place gives me the creeps," he said.

Soon enough the coroner made it official. John Krehbiel can't be *really dead* until the coroner says so, and then the attendants can wrap him up and cart him off. And then it's all over. And they're all gone, except me. There's nothing left in this empty house down at the end of a dead end street except me. I sit in silence waiting for the dead man's sisters to come; and I listen to the winter wind hitting the sides of the house until it seems to cry.

THE EMPTY CUBICLE

The cubicle was empty. The desk was stripped bare of the odds and ends that might give any clue as to the personality of the one who once worked there. Papers, pictures, pens—all gone. We knew that it was right to clean out his personal effects. You can't make a shrine out of old memories or they turn into ghosts and haunt you. Someone new would need the place and then he or she would bring their own things into this cubicle and make it their own. It would be a difficult assignment—to take the position of a fellow officer who just took his life. You can't make a museum out of an office, yet you can't deny the macabre reality of what this empty cubicle now represents.

Suicides are enormously complex. Survivors must process a bewildering array of feelings. A part of you hurts deeply as you feel the sorrow of accepting the sudden, unexpected death of a colleague. Another part of you is angry. One man's desperate act caused a lot of people to experience pain and that choice was selfish and unfair. The ones he loved the most were hurt the most. Another part of you feels compassion, knowing that no one makes such a choice unless they are desperate. Cops see themselves as courageous. They don't often admit that they hurt deeply or are confused. They don't readily admit that they sometimes need help. Until it's too late.

David's last few hours must have been dreadful. We will never really know what tormented thoughts tumbled about in his mind. The most we can do is try to understand what happened from the scraps of information and tiny clues he left behind.

Looking back it seemed clear that he had been lost in some unseen world of loneliness and despair. Some officers remembered how he made a few jokes about meeting for dinner and drinks next week. But they also remembered that he went home on Friday evening and wrote a simple but not very revealing note to his parents, telling them that he was sorry, but that the loneliness was unbearable since he'd broken up with his wife. They recalled that he then took his private back-up weapon, a small .357 magnum loaded with hollow-point shells, placed the weapon to his head and pulled the trigger. David's life ceased to be, in that dreadful moment in time when all his sorrow broke his heart and contaminated his thinking.

With one dreadful act, his life came to an end, and his family's life was sent into a bewildering spin of remorse, questions and agony. His police colleagues were left wondering what they could have done differently to have prevented this tragedy. And the shock waves of grief and guilt rumbled around the department like a prairie thunderstorm, leaving no one untouched.

I stood by the EAP officer, a commissioned and sworn officer himself, whose job it was to unravel the complex loose ends of this officer's disintegrating life and then help the deputies and office staff come to terms with the tragedy. He had to coordinate the memorial service, and to help offer hospitality to the dead officer's parents who came into town to gather their son's personal belongings and to walk one last time through his home and office to touch the places where only hours earlier he had walked. The EAP officer had to meet with his squad to give them the necessary details so that rumors and falsehoods might be kept at bay and grief might begin. Then he had to call me, the department chaplain, and tell me the story.

Telling the story to the sheriff, then David's parents, the squad, and then me made him touch the event again and again. It didn't get easier. To say to me, "Tom, we've had a tragedy. David has shot himself to death. We need you to come to the station to be with the deputies who found him and we need to tell his little boy what happened. And we'll need to do a memorial service when his parents come in. Can you help us?" That was very hard to do.

I remember the scene in that squad room as clearly as if I still stood there. Red-eyed officers, their faces ashen, stood together in a group. No one talked. Outside, in another room, David's son, a nine-year-old, sat with a family friend and his mother, as they all waited for me to find the right words to tell the boy that his father had just killed himself.

The little guy sat bravely in a chair with a Pepsi in his hand, and listened to me try to tell a truth no child should ever have to hear, while his mother and friends sat silently and tearfully nearby. For the rest of my life I will hear his mournful, bitter lament as he screamed in horror, "Oh, no! Oh, no! No, Daddy! Please!"

David's last act of kindness had been to send his son outside to play, lock the door, call his brother to tell him "Goodbye," and lay plastic sheets over the bed to contain the inevitable carnage. Beyond his personal terror, he did what he could to make it better for his friends and family. But it wasn't enough.

Funerals for those who commit suicide are hard to do. There was once a time when no one understood these tragedies. Family and friends were left with the dread that this loved one, lost in despair, overwhelmed by problems, and confused in his or her thinking, was destined to spend eternity in some state of unbearable, unrelenting horror. Suicide was seen as a sin for which one would be unable to ask for forgiveness

Most religious traditions see things differently these days. Now, more likely, we view such moments as impulsive acts or acts of desperation, but not ones that doom us to eternal damnation. It hurts badly enough to know a loved one made such a choice. Suicide can be contexualized as an act of sorrow and cloudy thinking, more than sin. and it is a time to remember that nothing can separate us from the love of God. Nothing. Not even suicide.

In such a funeral, the chaplain's responsibility is to try to understand the complexity of someone's life and then to summarize it in a few minutes of time, hoping desperately that we are honest without glossing over the painful reality of what happened and who this person was. We can't make them a saint. That never helps. Yet, we are all more than whatever human frailties come to light at our deaths. We are more than our secrets and we are better than our mistakes. And when the death is self-inflicted, the wounds the survivors feel are so raw and the consequences of the death so sharp that the pastoral task is especially complex.

Chaplains know very well that tragedies like this open pastoral doors that may have been previously closed. It takes a long while for chaplains to establish connections and build relationships with any law enforcement department. Some relationships don't develop until conditions are just right or not until we are called upon to offer a pastoral presence in a time of departmental crisis and offer comfort to bereaved colleagues in their grief. If we can help them find a semblance of meaning out of something that seems so senseless, then we can be certain that we have made a place for ourselves in the department.

A PROBABLE SUICIDE

"Tom, pick up 4571. It's 911. They said it's urgent." Our department secretary's message was crisp and to the point. Because we work at a level 1 trauma center, she is used to crisis calls. But until I came on the scene, she never got calls from law enforcement. She doesn't know what to make of the occasional requests to respond to an unknown problem. "They always sound so official," she says, and it unnerves her. But one thing she does know—something bad has happened.

I took the call and listened carefully as dispatch relayed the unfolding details: "Tom, need you to respond to the southbound rest area in I-135. We have a probable suicide. We believe the subject is still locked inside the cab of his 18-wheeler. Apparently his wife left him and he was despondent. He was staying with his parents and they thought he left on a trip to pick up a load of cattle, so they didn't worry for a couple of days. Then his supervisor called and asked if they knew where he was because he was a 'no-show' for the pickup. That's when his family got worried and notified us. They were the ones that found his truck. It's all locked up. The sheriff is asking if you can respond."

I started for Newton immediately. In this kind of work, you learn to set ordinary things aside in a hurry. As I approached the scene I tried to prepare myself for what I had to do. Chaplains most often are called to be present, to listen or to encourage healthy grieving. The old folk wisdom, "Don't just stand there, do something" is reversed for chaplains. "Don't do something, just stand there." Chaplains will tell you that standing alongside deeply troubled people is tough, and can hurt. I also tried to imagine the horror his parents must be feeling. No matter how old your children are, you never completely stop worrying about them. It must be embedded in the deepest part of a parent's genes. They can be adults with their own kids, but part of your heart will always be concerned about them.

When I watch a family disintegrate in grief when they hear the mournful news of an adult-child's death, it does weird things to my spirit. I have a lifetime of dreams for my own adult children. And now I have dreams for my grandchildren as well. I would spare them all from every heartbreak of life if I could. The thought of a tragedy harming them is too painful to consider.

Traffic was light so I made good time.

"Nine-o-nine to Newton." It was the on-scene deputy. I ride with him a lot. He's a friend as much as a colleague. His voice betrayed his anxiety.

"Go ahead, 909"

"Newton, if you can get 606, ask him to expedite. Family's here. We're keeping them a ways off. They're pretty upset."

"Ten-four, 909."

"Six-o-six, direct," I responded. "I'm about five out"

"Ten-four, 606. I'll be standing by with the parents at the north end of the rest area."

I could see the red lights of the deputies' cars and an ambulance, too. A small crowd of travelers who were at the rest area gathered in a grassy spot close to the restrooms and watched. Tragedies always draw the curious. Nine-fifteen's unit was a hundred yards away from the suspect's truck. Nine-fifteen had already wisely decided to maneuver the parents away from the truck under the legitimate guise of gathering information.

"Mom, Dad, this is Tom Shane. He's our chaplain. We called him to be here for you in case this is what we think it is."

Nine-fifteen was guarded and tried his best to tell the truth in a way that remained sensitive yet realistic. I thought his must have been the toughest assignment of all the deputies at this event. To wait with family while the inevitable bad news comes to light is to feel helpless. Cops are action-oriented professionals, but there are times when what is needed is patience and sensitivity.

"What's happening?" the mother asked me with a look of despair weighing on her face.

"I'll check in with the sheriff," I said. "He'll fill me in on everything and I'll report to you."

I noticed that neither parent asked to come with me. Somewhere inside they knew that a hundred yards away their once bright promise of a son was almost certainly dead.

I was caught off guard when I approached the truck. The sheriff and a few officers stood silently beside the truck. Standing on a small ladder, a man from Elden's Lock and Key worked to gain entry into the cab.

Then I saw it. Hundreds of flies hovered inside the cab. Probably thousands. Like a living black blanket, the flies covered everything. They were the harbingers of death.

When the lock was unsealed, the locksmith stepped aside. He knew his work was done, and he would not take the next step of opening the cab itself. He was as close as he intended to be.

The sheriff stepped on the truck's tiny footrest and opened the door. Instantly, a wash of hot putrid air rushed out and enveloped us with its foul odor. The smell of death was ominous in the Kansas August afternoon.

The sheriff shut the door and said to the undersheriff, "Call the coroner and get a unit to transport the body to his office. It's their job now. I won't ask any of you to remove him."

A hundred yards away and a short while later I stood with the parents as they watched from afar as their son was placed in a black body bag and taken away for an autopsy. The deputy said as kindly as he could, "It's better if you wait here. We can confirm that it is your son, and we have every reason to believe he took his life. He left a note. Technically it is a crime scene, so we'll need to officially investigate just to rule out foul play." He paused, not knowing how to continue with the rest of the story. I knew his dilemma and I detested it, too. I've worked other summer suicides and I know what happens to bodies left unattended for days. Death is always sad. Some deaths are worse.

The deputy continued, "You must understand that he has been here for several days and that has left him ..." He paused, trying to find the right words.

"I can imagine," said the father, interrupting the deputy. "We'll remember him as he was, not as he is now."

From a distance we watched as the coroner removed the body from the truck, zipped the black body bag shut, and loaded it into the ambulance. Both parents watched with sorrow etched in their faces, undoubtedly reflecting their spirits. Quietly I walked with them back to their car. My heart was sad. "I'm so sorry," I said.

They shook their heads and said simply, "Thank you." They asked a few procedural questions and I tried to determine what kind of support they had to rely on in the grief-filled days to come.

The afternoon sun shone relentlessly on the prairie. Not a breath of air broke the shimmering heat waves that hovered over the southbound rest area. The parents thanked us for the support the department made available, and for our kindness. They held hands as they walked quietly back to their car and drove away.

Pastoral care for chaplains in law enforcement is a ministry of moments. It is unlikely that we can make things right again. What we offer is a redemptive pastoral presence in which we stand beside people in their time of trial, believing that there is comfort and healing in this holy presence. We are a shoulder to lean on in this most barren of all moments.

Most often we know nothing about those whose lives cross ours in their time of tragedy. When the event is over, they slip away to their lives, and we may never see them again. But we remember.

MY GRANDPA DID THE SAME THING

I walked across the darkened backyard toward the tiny frame house. The moon cast pale shadows across the backyard. An autumn evening chill sent a shiver down my back. My jacket felt good, but I knew that the real reason for my shudder was less the autumn chill and more because I was walking toward a place where an unknown man had hung himself just hours ago. For one more time, as a police chaplain, I would enter the sad world of those who must contend with something as tormenting as a loved one's suicide.

Flashlights brightened the garage like little searchlights looking for secrets. I waited for the deputy to recognize me. He was young, and new to the department, but I had worked with him before. Inside, a detective snapped a picture and for one moment, every nook and cranny, every rafter and every ordinary tool was revealed in stark stillness. And so, too, was the ghostly silhouette of the lonely man who still hung from a beam. Once a husband, a father, a worker, a friend, a son, and a living human being, he was now a statistic. A memory. A quiet, broken dream.

For reasons now forever lost in death, this stranger made the unchangeable and devastating decision to end his problems by suicide. Tragedies like this never happen in isolation. They involve those who knew him best and loved him most … people who now grieve for their loss and who wonder what they might have done differently to have prevented this most perplexing of all deaths.

And suicides always involve law enforcement. Until otherwise known, such deaths are treated as potential crimes. In their own way, suicides bring a haunting, melancholy sense to the officers who must investigate them, take the pictures, and work with the families who endure the aftermath of grief and anguish. It is the silent part of police work that is too little understood or appreciated by the public.

The young deputy saw me standing in the driveway and greeted me. "The teenage son's inside the house. He found the body. When the kid came home from school he couldn't find his dad. Then, just before dark, he went into the garage and … He's pretty shook up. Can't blame him. His mom's in there with him now." With that brief review of the unfolding facts, the deputy turned to go up the back steps into the house.

"I'll introduce you, Tom, but then I've got to go," the officer continued. He then nodded back toward the garage. "They're about done inside and I'm afraid the coroner will ask me to help cut him down and I can't do that."

The young deputy stopped for a moment as if to steel himself against some silent but sinister threat. His features were blurred in the darkness, so I could barely see his eyes. But it was the catch in his voice that told the tale. "My grandpa did the same thing. I found him just like this kid did. I can deal with it up to a point, but I can't cut him down. Not again. I did that once. It's just too close."

Once inside the house, another kind of silence hung like despair. Mom tried her best to comfort the grieving son. The deputy put his arm on the lad's shoulder trying to convey with his touch a truth that words might never adequately speak: that the youngster was not as alone as he felt. That, in fact, someone else had stood in a moment just like this one. It was a truth I could never convey, however much I might want to bring comfort. I had never been in this circumstance; but the deputy had, and he summoned his own troubled memory and let it guide him as he reached out to the teenager in compassion.

A traumatized son, a grief-stricken mother, and an officer, all who had to face bitter memories. All were wounded in their own way and needed each other.

VII
DESPAIR

It was quiet in the large garage when I entered with a sheriff's deputy. A big Dodge dually was parked outside nearby, and the truck ticked softly as the engine cooled. Dust hovered in the air. Paramedics went about their tasks of taking pictures and writing reports with a somber professionalism. Those who talked at all spoke in whispered tones, not wanting to disrespect the scene. The deputy filled me in on the details of the tragedy, which were brutally clear and painful. It hurt to hear the story.

The driver had been backing his pickup into the garage with his young son riding in the bed of the truck. For reasons never to be known, the child tumbled out of the truck under the slow moving wheels. The dad didn't notice his fall until he felt the bump. In one tiny moment, life for the child, his dad, and the rest of the family was forever changed.

The man called 911 when he realized what had happened, and then sat beside the body of his child as the emergency responders hurried to the scene. Overwhelmed with grief, the father could not talk, and seemed to slip far away into a world of despair.

My heart ached as I knelt beside the grief-stricken man as he rocked back and forth on his back porch. Members of his church and neighbors rallied to his aid. He looked at me but saw through me to another world. Then it became clear to me. This is what despair is like. It is a moment with no hope. It is a time when all your dreams are destroyed. Time stands still.

Crisis pastoral care by its very nature is unsettling. It is inevitably grounded in broken dreams and human frailty, sin, injury, and illness. Probably no question haunts humankind more than why bad things happen to good people. This is crisis pastoral care in the raw. Chaplains may not have easy answers, but we can honor the question and offer ourselves to sit with those whose lives have been crushed to rubble. This element of pastoral care summons us to do what we can to find tiny pieces of hope so that those battered by misfortune can find a measure of healing beyond their despair.

If police chaplaincy is exciting for personal and professional reasons, so is it work that takes the chaplain into the depths of despair. One must be aware of his or her own private world, and where he is vulnerable to being overwhelmed, and what resources are available to meet the challenge. So must one know how to function in a crisis. Pastoral care in times of disaster requires special skills and education. Finally, one must conceptually understand a significant number of concepts—from the social sciences, to theology, to law enforcement policy and procedures—to function well.

WHEN LOVE IS NOT ENOUGH

Chuck had been a cop, and in many ways he fit the stereotype: big and strong, with cold eyes and stern countenance. That was before he experienced a call from God to enter the ministry. He went to seminary and was ordained. Now, this cop-turned-clergy was my student.

One day, as I entered the office, Chuck gave me the news: "Chaplain McClain from Newton Medical Center called and asked if you'd come down right away. She sounded upset."

With that information still fresh in the air, my pager squealed and the communications center more matter-of-factly announced: "Six-o-six, respond to NMC as soon as possible and meet 904 for an emergency." That was all I knew. My mind raced with questions and fears: "Why didn't they give me more information? Why did the hospital chaplain sound so upset? What if it was someone from my family?" My older son was on his way home from the University of Kansas so he and I could leave to go fly fishing in New Mexico that night.

But, having learned well the art of control from being around cops, I stuffed my dread, turned to Chuck and said, "Want to come along? It's a good chance to learn about crisis ministry first hand."

After a quick trip north, we arrived at the hospital and were met by 904. "Hell of a thing, Tom," the officer reported with quiet resolve. "Got a kid in the ER who's not gonna make it. He's just five years old and was at those people's house for a birthday party." With that, 904 nodded toward a couple sitting in the nearby waiting area. They were too young for such agony, but it was their destiny nonetheless. Wet and shaking in her misery, the young mother trembled all over. Her long brown hair lay matted over her shoulders. Her husband sat by her side, held her close and said, to no one in particular yet loud enough for all to hear, "Oh Jesus, this is so terrible!"

Nine-o-four continued: "They live on a farm just outside of town and were having a swimming party for their little girl and her friends. The mom over there counted heads, came up one short, looked in, and saw the kid on the bottom of the pool. No one knows how the other children didn't see him. Or the adults, either. You'd have to think it was only seconds that he was down, or the kids would've stepped on him or something. The mom jumped in, got him out and began CPR right away. Someone else called 911." The deputy stopped for a moment to let this sink in.

"Damndest thing, Tom," he continued. "The ambulance crew was all at the station for a meeting when the call came in and they were on scene within three minutes. Excellent response time. Mom had already started CPR. Another mom called 911. The ambulance got there immediately but not a damn thing worked. The kid's parents were called and are en route. They know something's up, but they don't know what. Tom, you gotta know this—their only other child died of leukemia a year ago. This one's gonna hurt like hell."

Sometimes the best thing and maybe the only thing to do is nothing. And so it was that Chuck and I stepped aside to let the event teach us. Off by a wall, the bewildered young mom all wet and shaking sat by her husband and cried from sorrow at the horror of it all. Here and there the nurses and other medical professionals touched one another in knowing sensitivity. One nurse walked about, her eyes brimming with tears. Pulling me aside, 904 said, "That nurse's little boy was at the birthday party. She knows the kid inside real well. She's glad it ain't hers, but feels all torn up because it's a family friend."

Sometimes, besides doing nothing but paying attention to the event to learn what needs to happen and who needs care the most, the most redemptive thing to do is something fundamentally practical. In a crisis, often as not the basics are overlooked. Drawing upon a dozen years on the Dallas Police Department, Chuck spoke to one of the nurses, pointing to the shaking woman whose clothes were still saturated from her rescue attempt: "Why don't you see if you can get her some scrubs. She's wet and cold and needs something dry."

Of course she did, but with the emotional energy directed across the hall, through the door, behind the curtain to the ER table where a little Code Blue boy lay slipping farther and farther away, things like dry clothes seemed a world apart.

Indeed, all our worlds were self-contained. And separate. Perhaps the pastoral task in such times is to make connections. To bridge emotional chasms. To arrange for warm, dry clothes. To touch crying nurses. Destiny sets its own pace and goes its own way.

When I heard the running footsteps down the corridor, I knew the little boy's parents were here. Oh, how I dreaded what was to come. There is little joy in emergency ministry.

There is nothing a pastor can do to make such a world right again. There is no easy healing of a broken dream or a dead child. There is no harder truth than to touch your dead child and feel his flesh grow cool. There is absolutely no stillness that is like the total quietness of your child's lips when you know that he will never again say your name.

To the frantic young parents the nursing supervisor so gently said, "We're doing absolutely everything we can. Our doctor has been on the phone constantly to Wesley Medical Center in Wichita consulting with their pediatrician. We're just not gaining ground. Maybe if you come in and speak to him it will help. Maybe some way, he can hear you and it will help." So much effort. So much care. So much mystery. And so much hurt.

And finally, it was over.

"I'm so sorry," said the physician. "I'm so sorry." With that, the truth of the flat monitor told what we all never wanted to hear. The child was dead.

Inside, I burned with grief. I was also angry at the unfairness of it all. As best as I could tell, no one did anything wrong. A family was devastated with grief because their child, their second child, was dead. Another family wept in despair because it happened at their home. And staff saw their best efforts fall short as their labor did no good.

I stood in the shadows of the emergency room curtain while mom and dad stood by their dead child. Standing by his head, the stunned mother stroked him in her own gentle way. The way she probably stroked him nearly every day of his life. She wiped his damp hair to the side the way it was always parted. A nurse gently removed the IV from his arm and put a bandage on his elbow so drops of blood would not show. His dad buried his face in the boy's chest and cried softly, "Oh Bud, I'm gonna miss you. Honest to God, Bud, I'm gonna miss you every single day for the rest of my life. Oh Bud, why'd it have to happen?"

"So faith, hope, and love abide, these three; but the greatest of these is love." (I Corinthians, 13:13). But sometimes there is not enough love to change the bitter realities of life. Love alone will not turn back the ravages of accident or illness. One only hopes that enough love can be scraped together to give away to those who hurt so horribly so that some day they will find enough healing to go on.

I excused myself for the moment and told Chuck I would return. Then, I walked down the hall to where my wife worked as a physical therapist. I needed to experience her love and concern to alter the sense of isolation I was feeling. I needed to make contact with those I love most, and to touch them. It changes nothing ... but still.

Later that night, with my oldest son home from the university, we drove west toward New Mexico in a driving thunderstorm, and I knew that I would treasure every moment of our lives together more than ever.

GUILTY OF FIRST DEGREE MURDER

After eleven long years of providing pastoral care every Friday afternoon in the Harvey County jail, the old jail had been replaced with a new state-of-the-art facility. The way into the jail was through a great iron door which was controlled by the communications center and monitored by a TV camera. Once inside, I would make a sharp right turn and walk down the long gray corridor past the solitary cells. Since the old jail was built of steel and concrete, sounds echoed off the floors and rattled between the walls and ceilings, and the iron bars holding the prisoners inside. After another sharp turn, I would enter a long corridor where most of the inmates were housed. Bits and pieces of broken hopes littered the way.

Behind these unyielding iron bars were those who had broken the law or were awaiting trial and now paid the price. I always tried to be careful there. It was a place full of complainers and manipulators who had learned to look with hard eyes at the world. It was a place where feelings were ignored and lives put on hold. Sometimes I would tell new pastors who wanted to work in the jail to see beyond the presented picture.

"Their stories will impact you," I told my students. "If you're not careful, you'll see them as people and not prisoners. You'll see past their glare and into their loneliness, past their sneer to their sadness, and past their bravado to their sense of guilt. And if you look too long into their eyes you'll see that in addition to a smoldering rage there is often a sense of shame and regret."

I tried to teach students to listen to the silence of the place. Beside the fact that the television blares all day and there are four inmates playing poker who josh around and curse each other as they pass the time, there is a silence that undergirds all that

112

clatter. This empty sound is much louder than the rip of a deck of cards or the lies and yarns of the inmates. It is the silence of the scream of their own mistakes or the thud of their dreams as they fall to the ground. To work in the jail is to ultimately face the truth that though we are separated from the inmates by iron bars, in some fundamentally human way, our lives are frighteningly similar.

***

The scorching southern wind blew like a raging prairie fire across the Kansas plains and howled outside my office window. I was on a long distance phone call when I was paged to call the communications center immediately. "Tom, the verdict is in on the Burnett case. They found him guilty of first degree murder," said the dispatcher. He went on to say that Burnett's mother was hysterical and grief-stricken, and the sheriff had asked that I be called to give some assistance to her.

Once at the jail, I walked past the brightly lit corridor where the trustee was watching television and sipping coffee. I stopped at the large iron gate and pushed the tiny black button that gave me access inside. I listened to the loud rumbling as the gate screeched open just long enough for me to enter and then just as coldly shut with a loud clang. Immediately to the right of this electric gate, I stopped and paused at the door of the solitary interview cell. For just a moment, I allowed myself to ponder the incident which called me here, along with the hardness of the jail itself. Jails are unforgiving. There is no softness anywhere. I opened the door to the solitary cell, peeked inside and saw two silent and very lonely people. The room was thick with smoke, and my eyes burned immediately. Mrs. Burnett chain-smoked one cigarette after another, as if that ritual would somehow soften the unbelievable tragedy that her son had been found guilty of first degree murder. Once inside, I introduced myself: "The sheriff asked me if I'd stop by and see if I could be of any help."

Randy Burnett reached out to shake my hand and his mother said softly, "Oh, yes, Chaplain, come in. Thank you for coming." Even in this grim hour, each managed to greet me with hospitality.

The feeling of despair was as heavy in that closed, solitary cell as the cigarette smoke that hung everywhere. Randy and his mother sat side by side and seemed unable to fathom the depths of the tragedy, which must have seemed like a bad dream from which they would awake. But this was no dream. This was a hard core reality that no hoping, wishing, or praying would change. Mrs. Burnett sometimes watched the blue cigarette smoke as it lifted into the far, dark corner of the small cell and vanished, and sometimes she looked at the floor and seemed to stare a hole through the concrete. Sometimes she reached over to Randy and held his hand. And always she wept. Her eyes were red from the bitter tears of anguish and disbelief, and the black mascara from her eyes slipped down along the creases of her face as her tears spilled down her weary cheeks.

What must it be like to be a mother who wanted desperately to believe that her son was innocent and decent and caring, but who had just sat through a trial in which he was accused of brutally and savagely murdering an old woman minding a convenience store?

"It can't have happened. Not first degree. I just don't believe it," she said to me, and probably to herself as well. "Randy's always been a good man. Oh, he had his scrapes, but never anything serious. He just couldn't have done this to a woman. He has always treated women well. Maybe he has had a few fights with guys, but he's never hurt a woman in his life. That's just not something he would do!" It is so hard for a mother to believe that her son is the savage killer he was found guilty of being.

Randy himself sat in his chair and looked the most unlikely person I'd ever seen to be a murderer. Short and slight in stature, he had an innocent-looking face and soft blond hair. He was dressed in the smartly pressed and stylish gray suit he wore in the courtroom, like someone who had just come from a job interview. The full weight of his predicament was almost more than he could fathom. He profoundly denied everything, and I think, in truth, he may not have known or believed that what he was found guilty of doing had actually happened. At least not by him. I had a feeling, at the time, that what he was found guilty of doing must have been so evil, and so absolutely unacceptable, that he had blotted it out.

As we talked he told me that he was given a first-degree murder verdict and that it would likely mean a life sentence. He sobbed. A flood of thoughts ran through my mind. I wondered if the family of the victim would care at all that he was distressed, when their own loved one had been so brutally murdered. I wondered what it must be like, on the other hand, to think about spending the rest of your life behind the unforgiving and uncaring iron bars of a penitentiary. I wondered what it does to one's own sense of life and destiny and values to know that you will live with that memory somewhere in your mind forever. I wondered what it must be like to know that for the rest of your life you will be living within a society filled with others who also made their own dreadful mistakes and where the sense of safety and security are so often compromised.

As I prayed with them for courage in the long and lonely days to come, and as I prayed for forgiveness for broken moments, and as I prayed for hope in the empty days ahead, both mother and son held hands and sobbed.

In time, Randy's attorney arrived, and I said goodbye. It was a sweet feeling of relief to know that I could get on the phone and dial a number and the big, iron-barred gate would open, because I had the power and authority to make it do so. Through the thick, steel door of the interview cell the muffled crying could still be heard, and the blue haze of cigarette smoke slipped through the tiniest of cracks and melted into the open spaces of the Harvey County jail.

THE ROAD TO OMAHA

From the top of the gentle hill I could see a man in blue jeans and a ball cap standing beside the red Grand Prix talking on a cell phone. "Car trouble," I thought to myself. I always feel guilty when I drive by stranded motorists. They could be sick, or injured. Whenever I pass by, I remember a time in 1963 when I saw a motorist off on the side of the highway in a driving rain storm near Emporia, Kansas, on US 50. I didn't stop then either. But I found out later that there had been injuries in an accident. Ever since then I always want to stop. But this man had a cell phone, so my sense of guilt was assuaged.

My wife and I had just crossed the state line on the way to Omaha. I was to be the guest speaker at a friend's installation service at the church to which he had been called. It was to be a fun trip for us. Already, the flat Kansas prairie had gently given way to rolling hills. Near the man on the mobile phone, a second man appeared and motioned for us to slow down. I hadn't noticed him at first. He looked worried ... maybe even frightened. Something didn't seem right. Speeding by at sixty miles an hour, these scenes, and the fleeting thoughts that unexpectedly emerge from instinct, only take seconds to develop. There is no time to process them. A hundred feet ahead of me, off on the shoulder, a semi-tractor trailer was parked ... an odd place to stop.

Then I saw more. Off to my right, on the dirt road that crossed the highway, an old green GMC pickup sat cross-wise in the road. Suddenly it was horribly clear what had happened. The frantic phone caller and the man waving his arms were pointing to an accident. Even before I stopped, I knew this was a horrible tragedy. The occupants of the battered pickup were too still. The truck was too battered. The bystanders were too frantic. The debris around the crushed truck was too scattered.

As a chaplain and a reserve police officer, it seems scripted in me to help. I never really know *what* I might do, but there is usually *something* I can offer. Sometimes people don't think of the most basic things. I could help direct traffic. Even a little warning would be a help. This road dipped down to the gentle creek bed below before rising back again. It's not much of a drop and it wasn't even dangerous. But when you are traveling at highway speed and suddenly come upon a tragedy, your attention is understandably captivated by the wreck.

I approached the shattered pickup truck. Bits and pieces of debris were scattered all about. Shards of glass littered the dirt road, blown out by the impact. Every window was shattered.

Inside, the driver, an old farmer, sat stunned and disbelieving. His head was cut. He looked through the empty windshield and seemed to stare past me into a lost world that I could not see. Gently and slowly, he rocked back and forth in the old truck. Softly he moaned, whether from pain or grief I could not tell. His gray striped bib overalls were covered with blood and pieces of broken windshield. The cut on his head dripped blood down his cheek and onto his overalls.

I called 911 and reported the incident, then tried to reassure the old man as best I could, "Help will be arriving shortly, sir, and we'll be here with you if you need anything."

I looked at the person beside him. Oddly enough, I couldn't make out the gender of the passenger, but guessed that it was a woman, his wife perhaps. She was still, and looked somehow oddly misshapen. I stepped closer. Standing only inches from her I could see why I had such a hard time being clear who she was and why she looked so odd.

A shiver went up my backbone. I looked again and confirmed what I didn't want to believe. The woman's face was gone. Her long hair hung where her face would have been, but it was a face that was battered and crushed beyond identification. Nearly torn off. I guessed she had taken the full impact of the tractor-trailer head-on collision and was crushed beyond recognition.

My heart went out to the old man, as I questioned to myself what had happened. I imagined all sorts of possibilities. Maybe he never saw the truck and turned directly in front of it. Maybe he didn't stop at the highway's edge and thought he was clear to cross. Maybe he saw the truck but thought he could beat it. A dozen maybes crossed my mind. But nothing changed the horrid reality. Another stranger happened by, a woman. She saw the same grisly scene and, without a word, she went to her car, found a blanket, and draped it over the body of the battered and broken woman.

Somehow it seemed a kind thing to do. It gave the old woman a sense of privacy and dignity.

"I'm a paramedic," said the first bystander, the driver of the red Grand Prix. "I didn't see it happen," he quickly explained. "At least I *used* to be a paramedic. I don't practice anymore. I'm into sales now. But she's dead. I checked her … no pulse."

The truck driver wasn't hurt, and it appeared to not be his fault. But he too was caught up in a moment bigger than he ever expected.

Way off in the distance I could hear the wailing siren, then the blinking red lights appeared a mile away. A local sheriff's officer arrived and made a quick overview before giving an updated and accurate assessment to the communication center.

Help arrived, and in droves. First the deputy, then a fire truck, then the ambulance, then two troopers. I could see four more marked units approaching before my wife and I left the scene.

In rural America, the sense of community is strong. When I first ran to the scene, another man had slowed down beside me and said, "Isn't that John Schmidt? Sure looks like his truck." I wondered who would not see this couple tonight. Perhaps they had children who waited for their arrival. Or grandchildren who delighted in the peculiar secrets that only they could share.

I thought of my own children and grandchildren and how important they are to me. I wondered what it would be like for the old man to live with the awareness that however innocent his driving error, it resulted in the death of his wife.

It was quiet as we drove on. You can't do this work and not experience the pain of the event. Each of us processed our thoughts in the silence of the darkening Nebraska evening. Here and there in small towns, Friday night football games were starting. People were happy. They had reason to be, most of them anyway.

There was a time in my career, when my family was younger, when I would come home late at night after working a tragedy. My family would be sleeping so soundly that they would not hear the garage door open or the squeak of the back door as I walked in.

Sometimes I would sit for a while and think. I take my family for granted. But on those nights, I would be aware that lives taken for granted, or even lives cherished, can vanish with no chance to say goodbye, or to say all the things you carry in your heart.

Usually I'd tiptoe quietly into each child's room and listen to the gentle, rhythmic sound of their deep sleep and give thanks. And if the tragedy was especially sad, or when my defenses were thin, I would step to their bedside and feel the soft skin of their faces as they slept.

And sometimes I would sit with my wife as she listened to my story. It helps to have a partner who knows you in your darkest days and who has a heart big enough to listen. If you do this work long enough, you will come to see how quickly, how completely and sadly, life can vanish. Life is never ours to own, it is a gift to us for a while.

VIII
NATURAL DISASTERS

Not all police work comes about because people violate laws. There are moments when, as a result of natural disasters, whole communities fall into disruption. In such times, those communities depend on law enforcement to be one agency that helps to hold the fabric of life together. Law and order, communications, search and rescue, are some of our expected tasks.

On March 13, 1990, the cool Kansas prairie was threatened by massive clouds that hovered low. Here and there folks sneaked a peek at the darkening southwest sky and then went back to work. When you live in Kansas, you learn to live beyond the inevitable anxiety of a "tornado watch." They come about as regularly as the seasons. The truth is, even the more serious "tornado warnings" are sometimes too readily dismissed. While a "warning" tells the somber truth that someone has actually seen a tornado in the area or one was spotted on radar, most of the time the worst that happens is that a few outbuildings on some farm are blown apart.

But not that day.

The report indicated that a large tornado had actually struck a portion of Burrton, Kansas, and was grinding toward Hesston. Knowing it would pass a few miles west of my home, I left work to check on my family. Driving along the interstate on a high bridge at mile marker 33, I could not help but feel the absurd paradox of driving in sunlight that peeked through openings in the clouds, while a half dozen miles west I saw a massive, black, swirling and raging wind storm! Where I was, it was pleasant. Not far away, was the most devastating monster I had ever seen. It looked like the evil mushroom of an atomic explosion. All around it dust and debris churned. I had never felt so insignificant in the face of such power.

Nearing my home, I heard a sheriff's deputy calmly report to the communications center, "Call Chaplain Shane. Have him come to Burrton. We have one Code Black." I trembled in anxiety and anticipation. I could hear the sheriff's officers, state troopers, and Hesston officers begin to offer pieces of information and the massive weight of this tragedy began to take shape.

"Newton, we've taken a direct hit. We need help!" reported a Hesston officer. So began the longest pastoral care week in my police chaplaincy ministry until I would later be called to the Murrah Federal Building bombing on April 19, 1995, and then the terrorist strike at the World Trade Center buildings on September 11, 2001.

Later that evening, many officers from neighboring towns gathered to provide assistance. I stood next to the undersheriff and it seemed poetically right that we met at a church for our assignments: "Your job will be to secure the area. No one is allowed in. There may be live wires down and some gas lines are ruptured. Watch your step. Don't smoke. And look for bodies in the trees."

I thought it strange that we were there to provide "security." What an odd way to describe our task. What kind of security can one provide when nearly everything is gone? And whatever security we offered surely was pitifully small and too late. Maybe it is inherent in the human condition to reach for "security" and to find comfort in whatever we think it is when we grasp it.

It is natural for us to do what we can to guard against the horror of life. We summon the most creative thinking among us and turn with almost religious fervor to faith, radar, and warning systems. We seek truth from medicine and science and, in a relative sense, we do draw comfort from the temporary reprieve they give us. And we smile in relief that sometimes we can hold back the force of terror. But only for a while.

The silent truth of any disaster is that it whispers to us that, at best, we only buy time. Perhaps we do well to live humbly and respectfully and acknowledge that there is, indeed, a reality bigger than us and beyond our reasoning to which we will ultimately answer. In the meantime, we need to remember that beyond our differences, we live together in a human community that transcends the artificial markings which too often keep us apart.

A FIELD OF BROKEN DREAMS

The next day, March 14, 1990. Though it was barely sunrise, the debris-filled streets were already heavy with victims and helpers. With only a couple hours of respite, and for some not even that, folks were already at the task of searching mounds of rubble in what had only hours before been their homes. A picture under a pile of soggy boards. An item of clothing wrapped around a denuded tree. Tools still sitting on a work bench inside the garage that had been blown away, leaving the work bench untouched. Anything that could be salvaged was eagerly grabbed. Hesston, Kansas: a proud, little town on the prairie. Burrton, Kansas: another modest village a few miles southwest, and dozens of farm homes in between. All were torn apart, leaving nothing but piles of broken dreams because of a massive tornado.

I needed to get a personal sense of the trauma. It's just the way I work best. So I left the command post in Hesston to walk the tornado's path through town and see for myself the stupendous power of such a storm. As I stood in the center of destruction, I listened to the soft weeping of those who had lost everything.

Entire homes were gone. Only pieces of walls stood over empty basements. A multi-colored tapestry of treasures littered whole blocks. Twisted bicycles, broken TV sets, crushed tables and chairs, soiled and soaked carpets and pieces of clothing lay huddled in wet heaps. Appliances were battered. Cars were ripped open. What had once been centers of warmth and love were splintered memories of houses. Bright shards of insulation hung like Christmas tree decorations from what remained of the trees that were also broken and twisted. A refrigerator was nestled in the fork of another tree. Nothing was the way it used to be. And nothing was recognizable. Old landmarks were gone.

Deep gray clouds hovered just overhead and a cold mist occasionally sprayed the devastation. The sharp north wind seemed to add one more injustice to the event. I scrunched deeper into my coat and walked on. At every turn, one more awesome surprise awaited me.

Tragedies are simply uncontrollable. There will never be enough warning to avoid them, nor enough wisdom to protect ourselves from them. And someday it may be our turn. What matters most is that, beyond it all, we care for one another.

Chaplains are present to take note of what is seen and to think both pastorally and theologically about the nature of disaster. Natural disasters awaken concerns of faith. People hunger to hear words of hope. They need the rituals of faith to remind them that beyond this destruction there can be renewal. I saw this clearly when I came upon a row of toppled oak trees that were nearby a line of weeping willow trees. Not nearly as tall or as strong as the oak trees, they nevertheless were able to bend with the wind and thereby withstand the destructive force of the tornado. They were stripped bare of their leaves, but they were intact. They would come to full life again one day. It seemed a wise lesson from nature—to learn to be flexible. To bend in order to survive.

In one backyard, halfway up in a tree lay the crumpled remains of a Volkswagen. Someplace else, a whole semi-trailer truck filled with grain lay upside down. Here and there, whole cars were tipped over as if the tornado mocked us all with its utter disregard for all that matters to us, and large buildings were crumpled as if they were fragile flower petals. I could not comprehend such brute force.

Nor could I fully understand how a town could be fine and then within seconds be in complete shambles. I felt as if I were following a trail into a mystery. Even so, as I walked among the remnants of people's lives, I knew a strange mixture of awe at the unyielding power of this storm and sadness as I looked around. Families stoically milled about their ruins trying to pick up the pieces and put even a little bit of their lives back together again.

In its own way, it was so overwhelming that it was impersonal, the destruction so massive and over-powering that it made no sense. What did make sense were the stories I heard of personal tragedy. Maybe it's always been true that the greatest deeds of all are those carried out by ordinary people who simply do their jobs in extraordinary circumstances.

As I walked about the fields of broken dreams, I remembered my own experiences of the night before. From the relatively high vantage point of Exit 33 on I-135, I had looked northbound on my way home and seen the massive, black, rumbling column of horror as it churned toward Hesston. Seconds later I had heard a deputy asking that I come to Burrton for a death. While on the way there, I watched as the sky once again deepened and another ominous, low mass began to circle and seethe overhead. One more time, the angry heavens spit forth their fury and shredded everything, as a second tornado twisted through.

Later as I drove toward this second tornado to help track its path, I heard 918, Steve, on the radio: "When you have time, would you have someone check my home? I think it took a direct hit. I'll continue to check other houses in the path." He spoke so matter-of-factly; I couldn't believe he might have lost everything.

Indeed, Steve's home was destroyed. Totally. Every piece of it had been scattered into the adjacent fields and nearby woods. "It's OK to write about this, 606," Steve said, "just as long as you don't make it into something it isn't. I'm just a regular guy doing my job. And anyway, even though I knew my home was gone, I knew my family was out of town and safe. I don't really know what I'd have done, though, if they would've been there. I'm sure I would've gone home to be with them instead of working." Maybe so, but who could have blamed him?

Tragedies are all so unique and the individual resources of people are equally so personal that comparisons are pointless. But to lose everything one owns surely stands as monumental as any loss. So it was for 918 and hundreds of others that March day in 1990. In the twinkling of an eye, the dreams of years came crashing down.

There were others in law enforcement who worked even though their lives were battered and bruised, too. Troopers from afar were present within hours. Officers from other cities were dispatched to help. The National Guard answered the call. And hundreds of unknown volunteers offered support to a little Kansas town as trees and boards and bricks were hauled away so new lumber could be delivered and the re-building process could begin.

SHARING OUR STORIES

A half-dozen firefighters sat around the coffee table with me in a break room at the back of the fire station. Outside, the north wind blew sharply and a light rain dampened our spirits as well as the ground.

Barely twenty-four hours after the tornado, and with only a few hours of sleep stolen from our work to give enough respite to carry on, the firefighters and I melted into the silence of the night. I looked around the room and felt the weight of all our sadness. It's after the drama, when the adrenalin rush fades, and the energy born of search and rescue work is depleted, that one attends to his or her own thoughts and listens to the secret memories that have not been crafted into words. These are the lonely times.

"You know, I watch the troopers as they work," said one volunteer firefighter. "They're all strong and professional. Their uniforms are clean and they look like nothing bothers them. But I'll bet there's a soft spot inside them just like inside me. I've never seen this kind of horror before. I mean, it hurts me down deep inside." Indeed it does.

"When the warning came," he continued, "I knew *something* had to be done, so I took the fire truck and drove up and down the street with the siren screaming and me yelling over the loud speaker to take cover. And you know what? I didn't think anything about it at all until I drove by my own house!"

"My own house," he said again. And with that the room grew still. The firefighter looked down at the floor while the others looked away from him to respect the crack in his voice and the tears that slipped from the edges of his deep-set, sleep-starved eyes and melted into the bristles of his beard. For a long time, it was quiet. Each one of us remembered people we loved who we also left behind when we answered the call to come and help.

"The hardest thing I've ever done in my life was to drive right on by my house where my family was, knowing all the while that a tornado was on its way and they might be blown away without me there, and they might be killed because I wasn't with them. I was so scared for them. I knew if I stopped to be with them, I'd feel guilty, but if I drove on and did my job, I'd feel guilty for that, too. I decided to drive on, but I wanted so much to be with them."

The stillness of the room was broken again when I finally offered my own perspective. "I felt the same way, Chuck. I left my child at home and answered the call to go to Burrton. But when I got home, I knew how much I had upset my family. When I went to bed my little girl had left me a note on my pillow that said, 'Dear Daddy, I'm glad you're back. You had me so scared and worried. Love, Sara.'"

With massive losses all about and so many hurt so deeply, it is likely that such private acts by ordinary people will never be known. Sometimes it's enough to know in your heart that what you did in private helped strangers.

ROAD CLOSED

I parked on the shoulder of the county road just ahead of the steel guard rail over the bridge. The muddy current lapped underneath the bridge and swirls of debris floated downstream. Heavy rains had drenched the region for days. Every creek had turned into a torrent which then overfilled into the little creeks and they, in turn, surged across the fields and swept them clear of top soil.

When I drove down this same road the day before, 915 and I watched as tiny fish swam in the water-covered roads as if the very boundary of the rivers and streams had been obliterated, which indeed they had. Everything was topsy-turvy. Fish lost their bearings and swam in water which overflowed onto roads. With the rain soaking the prairie in cascading sheets that made visibility impossible, even prudent driving was risky. And if you disregarded common sense, you could be in trouble. The entire county was under a flash flood watch and 915 and I sat in his car and turned away travelers who wanted to risk passing through the rising waters.

Nearby, the wooden barricades and flashers across the road silently but clearly warned everyone to go no farther. "Road Closed" it said in plain letters. You couldn't miss that stark warning. But, not far from the bridge, a Toyota pickup lay empty in a nearby field.

For reasons that will never be known, a young woman had made the choice to drive around the barricade … and two previous barricades as well … and had tried to drive her Toyota truck across the swiftly moving current, which was perhaps a foot deep. The little truck and her inexperience were no match for the surging flood water. In some nighttime scene, which must surely have been one of devastating panic, the truck was swept off the road and began to float away, spinning madly in the swiftly flowing water and coming to rest in the middle of a field mired in several feet of water. The driver, perhaps hoping to find her way to safety, or perhaps never having a chance in the raging water, was carried away in the darkness in a manner known only to God and the thick darkness of a stormy night. The young woman was believed to have drowned and dozens of rescue workers were looking for her.

Not far off the county road in a grove of cottonwood trees, I approached a band of deputies, troopers, and paramedics as they tried to dissuade the missing woman's young fiancé and her father from striking out on their own across the muddy field into the soggy river bottom. They were desperate to help find their loved one. "We don't need to lose any more people," the sheriff responded as calmly as he could. "We have trained people working systematically to look for her and if you get in trouble it will only make things worse." When they persisted he added, "It's not safe. We'll inform you immediately when we know anything."

His logic was met with an unexpected rage by the fiancé. His forefinger thumped the chest of the sheriff to make his point. I watched as the nearby officers stood ready to arrest the bereaved man if he persisted in pushing the limits when he told the sheriff, in the most offensive language possible, that the rescue workers were idiots, and the sheriff was a fool, and they could do a better job themselves. And all the rest could "Go to hell."

You could see the sadness in their eyes and hear the horror in their enraged voices as they demanded to know why more wasn't being done. They wondered why the search party waited so long to get started. Why there weren't more searchers scouring the fields and wooded banks of the river. Indeed, they screamed in rage at the sheriff, who tried to address their concerns with patience and prudence only to be met with a scowl and a torrent of bitter profanities.

Grief does strange things to people. Judgment gives way to panic. Reason loses ground to passion. It takes a well-centered and wise officer to realize that he is dealing with grief and not malice and, therefore, not personalize the outpouring of anger.

Nearby, the Salvation Army had a table spread with fruit, cups of juice, and hot coffee. Rescue workers huddled together to share information and seek some comfort from the cold weather. It was difficult to walk knee deep in bone chilling water with mud sucking at your boots with each step. It's frighteningly unnerving to sit in a small boat searching in silence for a body which may surface at each turn around a bend, or even hang grimly from the branches of a tree, as the swirling waters recede and you pass nearby.

Searches take time, and the waiting is endless for both family and rescuers. Other family members arrived and gathered beside a waiting ambulance, its engine still running and serving as an unexpected source of warmth to those who sat together closely, nearby, in the raw winter afternoon.

"This is our chaplain," said the sheriff, hoping that a pastoral presence might offer some comfort and hope to the anguished family. Sometimes it helps. Sometimes people can rally around the possibility that faith may keep hope alive and that beyond all reason, maybe a miracle could happen.

The fiancé looked at me with bitter eyes and contemptuously dismissed me. For just a moment, I thought we stood at some crazy crossroad where the grieving man seemed to contemplate lashing out in rage—at the sheriff or at me. Though nothing was ever said, it was almost as if *somebody* had to pay for this tragedy. In such times, those who try to help are the ones held accountable—even though logic and common sense tell a completely different story. She was the one, after all, who crossed the barricades and entered an area known to be treacherous and, in so doing, paid the ultimate price.

But then the anger faded. The moment passed. The clenched fist softened and the victim's fiancé and her father wandered off alone into the dull, brown fields.

The afternoon wore on. The wind thickened with a heavy mist and dampness covered our bodies and our spirits.

And then it was over.

The victim was found, face down and buried in silt and still submerged in water. I stood with the sheriff as he graciously told the family the truth they dreaded to hear, but had long since come to expect. Fear had given way to relief. The expressions of anger softened and apologies were given—genuinely and with regret. They were accepted with understanding. When you work human tragedies enough times, you begin to understand that in the blindness of a moment things are said that are later regretted. The wise officer learns to hear the language of grief and fear and set it in context.

"We want to see her!" the family insisted.

Such a thing is always complicated. Unattended, suspicious deaths always hold the possibility that what happened was no accident after all. What seems so may not be. There are times when what you feared to have been a tragic accident turns out to be a malicious trauma. And all of that has to be sorted out.

But alongside the legal bewilderment of such mysterious deaths are the compassionate needs to care for survivors. When they see for themselves the reality of the event, it helps them heal.

One by one the family gathered at the local funeral home to identify the remains. Good-byes are always hard. Final good-byes hurt most of all. One by one we filed into the viewing room where the sheriff and the detective stood silently beside the black body bag, half open, with the woman visible enough to be seen and identified.

Ultimately, police work is people work. It's not just crime and courts or offenses and offenders. Often as not, it is work with deeply broken people who must endure the awful truth that a loved one has died an untimely and horrible death.

"I'm sorry I was so loud-mouthed out at the creek. I was just upset," said the woman's dad softly to me. He looked down at the floor as he spoke. "I apologize."

"I understand," I said, and touched his shoulder. I am so sad for you and your family."

One by one we walked out of the room back into a busy world which seemed unaware of the tragedy just witnessed by a family, the rescue workers, and the officers. But those who were there understood, and were marked by the wonder of it all.

IX
DEATH NOTIFICATION

The gray haired, middle-aged woman sat on a chair in the trauma waiting room anxiously hoping to hear from the physician about her husband's condition. She gripped her hands together, trying to stop her nervous trembling. Brought in by ambulance with chest pains in the early morning hours, he was rushed immediately to a treatment room where a medical team began working, trying to save his life.

"Oh dear God," she said mostly to herself. "Please let him be OK."

I was the duty chaplain for the day and my task was to sit with her and provide both information and support. Sometimes I would return to the treatment room and learn some new information that might help her manage her fear. Factual information keeps realistic hope alive and prevents false hope from taking root. And sometimes there are painful realities that give early clues that this will not be a happy ending.

It is a sacred task to sit with strangers in a bizarre new kind of intimacy known in few other places. In this event, I was caught between competing professional protocols. I already knew that her husband had died, but I was waiting for the attending physician to reveal this to the anxious wife. In this hospital, it was the physician's responsibility alone to inform family members of the death of a patient. It was neither the nurse's job nor the chaplain's. The longer the physician delayed in communicating this terrible reality, the harder it would be. I had already told the charge nurse that the victim's wife was beside herself with anxiety, and that the physician needed to tell her the truth.

Finally, as the doctor came into the room, the wife jumped up and demanded, "How's my husband doing?" Instead of directly answering her question, however, the physician withdrew into his medical comfort zone and began asking medical questions.

"When did he first start having chest pains?"

"After supper last night," said the wife. "How's he doing, doctor? Will he be all right?"

The physician asked more medical questions as if needing to know how to help the patient.

Finally the woman persisted. "How is my husband?" she demanded.

"Well," said the physician trying to warm to the task of truth telling, "your husband has experienced a situation that is incompatible with life."

She looked at him with a bewildered look on her face. What on earth did he mean? "A situation incompatible with life? So is he gonna be OK?"

The physician stood there seemingly unable to tell the truth in a clear and direct manner.

I couldn't stand it anymore, so in spite of the official protocol, I said to the confused wife, "The doctor is telling you that your husband has died."

With the crystal clear news now plainly revealed, she sat down in the chair, buried her face in her hands and wept.

In truth, the physician was an honorable one. He was competent. He cared about his patients. He had the respect of the staff. But like so many professionals, he was unable to plainly, directly, and compassionately give this very difficult news.

There are differing protocols among institutions and professionals about whose job it is to give death messages, but frequently in law enforcement it is the chaplain's job to learn the art of delivering death messages. It is never easy. It is never just a job. It is a necessary task that must be done with compassion and directness so that those who must hear this news and live with it will do so with hope.

Such news must be given in a timely fashion and in a clear, direct way so that there is no confusion. It is a difficult calling to be the bearer of bad news. Survivors will always remember this moment, who told them the worst news they will likely ever hear, and how it was done.

Giving a death message is as much an art as a science. The stories that follow show how difficult this task is. If not done in a compassionate way, the necessary grief work will be compromised. While delivering a death message cannot be done by following a simple formula, there are nevertheless several guidelines which are helpful, and these are pointed to throughout these narratives.

No one who works in law enforcement or ministry can avoid dealing with death. It is part of the job, and sooner or later, every police chaplain will have his or her turn to deliver the death message. For many officers or chaplains, it is a task that will be done because it *has* to happen, but it is always one of the most difficult and despised parts of the job. If I hear one comment more than any other it is, "I don't see how you do it, Chaplain. I hate delivering death messages. I'm glad we have you to do it." And I'm glad, too, because as unpleasant as it is to perform, it *is* necessary and it *is* an opportunity to bring hope and healing to the survivors at precisely that moment when they feel more despair and anguish than they have ever known or likely will ever encounter again.

There is no one right way to go about it, but it must be done with as much care and sensitivity as possible. The circumstances each chaplain will encounter will vary, the details will differ, and the way each chaplain works will be unique to him- or herself. One must begin with the realization that while delivering a death message is clearly a task that must be done, it is also true that a chaplain will be entering the most precious part of another's life—that dimension in which they love and care for another. Hearing the news, that a loved one is dead and that death occurred in an unexpected and likely violent manner, will hurt them deeply and scar them forever. The chaplain will not cause this suffering, but will be bringing this reality home to them. So we must appreciate what it is that we will do. When we enter a family's apparently stable world, the news we carry will shatter it to pieces.

The task of death notification must be done with love. If you do it and are so detached and so steeled that it does not touch you, then you simply do not understand what it is that you are about. On the other hand, because it is not your loss, you should be better able to keep your professional presence, and thus do the job with skill. My hope is that you will not allow your professional sense to crowd out your compassion, and that you will not escape untouched.

PREPARING FOR GRIEF

The trooper with me had never made such a call before. They told him in training he would have to someday, and that day had come. With his anxiety obvious, he asked me, "What do you want me to do?"

"Just be there. Stand beside me. I'll break the news. Just be available to answer their factual questions. They'll have some. They always do," I replied.

"K-710 and County 606 are 10-23," said the trooper on his radio as we pulled to the front of the house. Funny how long the fifteen-yard walk up the sidewalk to the front porch seemed. "You ready, K-710?" I asked.

"I guess," he replied, wishing he were somewhere else.

We stopped long enough to look through the front door window, down a hall, and into the kitchen. Two children were spreading peanut butter on crackers and teasing one another. The younger sister squealed in delight as her brother taunted her. The kitchen seemed filled with love. I rang the doorbell and watched as the kids came together to answer it. The door opened, and for an instant, I looked into the faces of the two children. They glanced first at me, then at the trooper, standing there in his crisp uniform and hat. And because it was night time, their mother was right behind them. Long before a word was spoken, there was an ominous silence. I saw it in every eye. Fear covered their faces. Why is a trooper here, tonight? And who is this stranger with him? And I know they saw something in our eyes, too, because eyes tell stories that words cannot frame. Surely they sensed that we brought dread, not gifts.

"Yes?" said the mother. "What do you want?"

"My name is Chaplain Shane. This is Trooper Williams of the highway patrol. We're looking for Mrs. Smith. We have some information to give her." I learned early on in my career that those who answer doors may not be the family members at all even if it is the right house. Or sometimes the family we're looking for has moved. Terrible news must be given to the right people—not neighbors, or friends, or guests.

"I'm Mrs. Smith. What's wrong?" It was a demand as much as a question. Even in those few seconds I could see her panic mount.

"Ma'am, we have some information to give you. May we come in?" If possible, I want to talk in a setting where communication is more personal, where I am more available, and where I can better sense what I need to do. Giving bad news on front porches between screen doors or over telephones is far from ideal. Besides, I believe this extra time involved in bringing us inside lets family members brace themselves inside their hearts for the news they fear is coming. A too sudden sharing can be overwhelming so I prefer to be in the home.

"Come in. Is something wrong? Is it my husband?"

"Yes, ma'am, I'm afraid we do have some difficult news to tell you."

My preference is to begin by letting the family know that what they fear is true—that I bring dreadful news. This also lets them start to prepare themselves. Sometimes people tell me, "Wait! Let me get my son (or daughter, or husband, or wife)." Something as bad as they dread must not be heard alone.

Once they know something bad is coming, and have braced themselves, the best way to proceed is directly. "There has been a serious accident in the county. It involves your husband. Mrs. Smith, I am so sorry to have to tell you that he was killed."

And all of a sudden, for a moment in time, all of life stopped. We stood there while the whole world shrunk to a space no bigger than a capsule that engulfed the trooper, the mother, the two children, a cat, and me. Nothing else mattered. There was no wider world.

Even now, years later, I still hear the screaming of the children in that part of my memory where I store such moments of great sorrow. It is the place deep within me where I have filed away other terrible memories, and the stories of suffering I have heard over and over again in a career of crisis work.

"Oh Daddy, oh Daddy, no. Not my Daddy," screamed the little girl. And I wished to God that it was not so, but it was.

She dashed back to some hidden room and found a teddy bear. A warm, fuzzy, always-smiling, always present teddy bear. Then she ran in a circle from the living room, to the dining room, down a hall, and back to the kitchen screaming in grief and begging for her father. The bear clutched in her arms.

The pre-teenage son stood in front of us with a look of bewilderment spread across his face. He withdrew into a private world where no one could enter and paced up and down the hall speaking softly to himself: "I can't cry. Not now. I'm the man of the house. I can't cry. I have to be strong."

And the wife was overwhelmed with the burden of grief as well. "Oh Jesus, Oh God. Oh Jesus, Oh God. Oh help us. Oh please help us." It was the despairing wail and heart-felt prayer of a young mother and wife who was suddenly and unexpectedly a widow. But then her countenance changed, and we knew she was in deep shock when she said, "Oh my! Where are my manners? Sit down and I'll make tea."

In one moment their whole world was ripped to pieces and nothing made sense. Except, of course, the absurd attempt to do something tangible, something that worked, something they could control, like boiling water for tea or clinging to a teddy bear.

LOOKING BACK

Class wouldn't start for fifteen minutes, so I chatted with the regular instructor as students drifted in after lunch. I was a guest lecturer at a small liberal arts college in Wichita. The topic I was asked to address was critical incident stress management, with a focus on my work at the World Trade Center. Off to my side a young coed stood silently. When another student approached the instructor and asked her a question, the shy coed saw her opportunity to approach me and said, "Dr. Shane, do you have a moment?"

She was young, had an armful of books, and had a pensive look to her face. I was surprised that she knew my name. I tried to remember a connection with her, but I drew a blank.

"Of course," I said, with my own curiosity now high. She moved into a corner of the room for privacy. I followed her, wondering what she wanted to say that needed to be done away from other people.

"I know you don't remember me, but I remember you. My name is Alice Emerald. You came to my house one spring evening about thirteen years ago to tell us that our dad was killed in a wreck. You said he died while trying to save someone else who was in the accident. Do you remember when you did that?"

She paused for a moment, looking at me, waiting for my response. Her eyes were clear and her voice strong, but it was obvious that the memory and its profound sadness still evoked a sense of great sorrow. Deeper than her words, I felt the raw edge of lingering sadness—sadness that started when she was a child and, though mostly resolved, was still a factor in her life. All of a sudden I *did* remember her—that crisp spring night ... this suddenly devastated family—with painful clarity. I could see her, with her mother and older brother, standing just inside the doorway of their home, a home only a block from ours, as she trembled in horror as I told them the worst news they would ever hear. She was the "teddy bear child."

Her dad had been killed in a truck accident. The collision ruptured some chemicals, spewing a toxic cloud of poisonous gasses which engulfed the accident. He had tried to rescue his partner, but was overcome and subsequently died.

The young coed smiled and brought me back to this moment. "I'm OK now. It was a long time ago. I want to thank you, Dr. Shane, for your kindness. I know it was hard for you to tell us."

I was stunned. After all these years, for both of us, really, in quite different ways and for quite different reasons, this old memory had lingered, never far away. Then she smiled again, turned, and took her seat at the back of the lecture hall.

Almost immediately, and quite unexpectedly, another young woman approached me, and surprisingly asked me the same question: "Dr. Shane? Do you have a minute before class starts?"

"I know you don't remember me," she began softly, "but our paths crossed fifteen years ago this spring when you came to Peabody with deputy Van Rossun to tell us that our mother was killed on US 50 in the construction zone. She was on her way to work in Wichita. It was foggy and another car crossed the center line and hit her head on."

For the second time within minutes, I was summoned back in time. My favorite author Frederick Buechner calls the place where you store old memories a "Room Called Remember." I love that phrase because it so clearly describes how I manage so many of my own life's stories. Of course I remembered this tragedy. It was a damp, drizzly morning with fog so thick you could barely see a car's length ahead of you and I went with the deputy the sixteen miles from Newton to Peabody to wake up a sleeping family. And, once again, I was destined to be this bearer of bad news.

"I want to thank you for being there. Even though you told us awful news, I could tell you cared."

Two different tragedies, two different families, two death notification calls, and then one day almost two decades later we were all together in the same room, at the same time.

Death notification is not just a job. It cannot be reduced to a few techniques which can be learned and then applied. It requires the willingness to encounter strangers in a time of horror, and to walk with them into their own "dark night of the soul," when their world is suddenly broken . You can't stop the anguish, but you can do your part with compassion so that the healing they so desperately need can begin.

I was glad the two girls remembered my presence and were kind enough to mention it. Unlike my demeanor with them, there probably were other times when I got lost in my own world and could not offer care with the level of compassion that was needed; occasions when I may have made a difficult event even more painful.

IT'S HARD WHEN IT'S A KID

"Park your truck behind the sheriff's unit," said the deputy, pointing to a group of patrol vehicles stationed by the water's edge. His tone of voice had none of the usual friendly, casual conversation that marked our relationship. With those instructions I drove down the dirt road, made a sharp U-turn and stopped behind 901's Black and White. The sheriff stood nearby with a couple of other deputies and the fire chief. I couldn't tell what they were talking about, but the fire chief was pointing out into the lake where his men were working. A look of pensive sorrow marked each one's face.

Emergency workers are used to working dreadful events, like this one, and they learn how to push back the distressing human feelings that accompany such moments to do their job, but those feelings never go away. They recede into the innermost hiding spaces of the heart, waiting to be acknowledged when the task at hand is over. Delaying our own grief buys time, but it doesn't resolve the pain. And this grief is hardest of all when the tragedy involves a child. Somehow we get used to working tragedies with adults, but never with children.

A hundred feet away I could see four firemen from the rescue unit wading chest deep in the water. Each one wore a black body suit and carried heavy grappling poles, which they systematically raked across the bottom of the lake just below the dock. No one smiled.

Dispatch had called me a half-hour earlier with the chilling news of this event. "Tom, we need you at East Lake, A-S-A-P. We have a five-year-old child missing. He's presumed drowned. Kid's mom is there and is panic-stricken. Sheriff wants you as soon as you can get here."

I carried that thought with me as I drove. I have a five-year-old grandson and the thought of something this horrible happening to him sent waves of sorrow and dread washing over me. In a few minutes, I would sit with a horrified mother who was hoping and praying for a miracle, but was steeling herself against the worst news she could imagine.

As I stood silently beside 901, the fire chief finished talking. "We've got Wichita's Water Search and Rescue here. Our men will work the area around the dock; their divers will search the bottom. If he's there, we'll find him."

The sheriff nodded in agreement and turned to me with details. "A five-year-old boy was fishing with his brother. The brother went in to the bathroom and when he came back, the kid was gone. No one saw him fall in but we have to assume that's what happened. Mom's up there on the picnic table. The older brother told her he was missing. She ran to the lake, jumped in the water to look. She spent maybe ten minutes. Then she called us and we started the search. But it's been three quarters of an hour and if he's in the lake, he's been down too long. We've moved from rescue mode to recovery. I've had deputies and volunteers search the shore in case he wandered off, but we found nothing. We've searched every trailer in this area in case he wandered into one of them, but he's not there. It doesn't look good. Mom's up there with some friends."

I walked slowly from the dock and stepped under the yellow tape that had been strung around the patrol cars and trees to keep other campers away. It also kept back the gathering news media with their cameras. They had picked up the news on their scanners and came for the story. This *was* news, but the terrified mother deserved her privacy, so the media were kept some distance away behind the trees.

I introduced myself to the young mother who stood by a concrete picnic table next to her camp trailer. Her wet clothes stuck to her and she shivered as much from fear as the cool fall afternoon. When I told her I was the chaplain, I could see the look of apprehension mark her face with terror. It happens a lot that way. In a time of crises, people associate the chaplain with bad news because so often we are a part of the comfort offered when something catastrophic happens. But it's not always so, and it's not all we do, so I reassured her that I was here to care for her and to help her wait for answers in this critical time, but that right now, there was nothing to report. I promised to be available to her and to serve as a liaison with the rescue unit.

Chaplains have the opportunity to connect with virtually every facet of a tragedy: the anxiously waiting family members, the law enforcement units, the fire-rescue units, even the press and the county officials. Sometimes that's what we do best: we connect with the entire system, listening, offering hope and encouragement, setting boundaries, and making practical suggestions.

Everyone else involved in a tragedy has something to do. The chaplain's primary task is to be present. We help make the system work more effectively. We are there to wait with terrified family members, to listen to them, to encourage them. But waiting is burdensome. It means listening to horrible fears and the outpouring of sorrow and grief as parents review what happened and ruminate about everything that went wrong, looking for blame or hope in all sorts of places.

Watching the mother shiver in the fall afternoon, I suggested to one of her friends that she take her into her trailer to change clothes. It was so hard to think practically and so unnerving to *not* watch the rescue operation that she had remained in her soggy clothes, shivering but unaware of her discomfort. It seemed to help to have something to do.

Family members hunger for information and one thing chaplains can do is stay connected with all the working units. It is imperative that chaplains know the personnel and have at least a conversant knowledge of the necessary tasks that each are responsible for. While we can be on-scene, where we offer support to the personnel directly involved in the operation, we should know when it is advisable for safety or legal reasons to respect the boundaries. Support for law enforcement and firefighters is crucial. They have the "hands on" work to do which is both dangerous and unsettling. On-scene support work involves encouragement. The time to process comes later. And a chaplain being there lets other team members know that we *do* have a certain level of engagement; we *do* understand the raw pain of the event; we are there to care for *them* as much as we are present for the victim's family members. As we gather pertinent information about how the rescue or search operation is unfolding, we help keep family members informed.

I walked slowly back to the dock where the fire chief greeted me. "Here's the plan, Tom. My men are searching here. Wichita Search and Rescue has divers combing the bottom. There isn't much current down there, so if he's there, it is just a matter of time until we find him. When we do, I will put out a call on the radio and that will be the signal. Then we'll package him and put him in the ambulance and take him in. Mom won't have to see him."

I knew the chief meant well, because I've worked with him before. But his attempt at kindness ran counter to what the mother needed. Cops and firefighters often want to protect parents from experiencing more grief by shielding them from the painful truth that their child is dead. To see their child—perhaps ravaged by an auto accident, or shot in a hunting accident, or burned to death in a fire—is to hold the horror in your heart and feel its pain all over your body. Rescue workers would protect the parent if at all possible. It comes from their compassion, not from any insensitivity. Some would argue for this practice, but such protection is probably less useful than commonly thought. And family members should at least have the choice. Better the parent face the reality of death, because the truth is the doorway to healing.

In that moment I became the mother's voice. "Chief, Mom has asked that if we find him, she be allowed to see him. And I think that would be most helpful."

He paused briefly, seemed to be thinking about my observation, and then said, "OK, but will you be with her in the ambulance? I don't want her to be alone."

"Yes," I said simply. "I'll be with her." Being with grief-stricken parents when their child dies is familiar ground for me. It is a sad part of my regular job as a pediatric chaplain in the hospital where

I work. I have done it for years, but it is never routine. My heart is saturated with the mournful wailing of those whose souls cry out in their anguish and their sadness. But of all times, this dreadful moment is when chaplains are most needed. It is where I choose to be. And in spite of commonly held belief, it is a time to be silent and to listen, not to give advice. This is a ministry of presence that transcends race, gender, culture or religion. Such witnessing presence is a fundamentally human experience offered by a person of faith.

Not long after our conversation, the dreadful coded message came across my radio. The child was found. The chief approached me, "We've got him, Tom. We'll wrap him in blankets while you get Mom." He looked sad.

Although it was only fifty yards to the picnic table, too far away for Mom and her friends to hear any words, they were close enough to watch the rescue activity and to observe the serious conversation between rescue workers. Perhaps our slow pace as we approached alerted them. It may have been the look of overwhelming sadness on my face. The closer the detective and I got to the mother, the more she screamed, "Oh my God, No! No! No! It can't be! Oh my God No! Tell me it's not so!"

But it was. Before I said a word, the mother intuitively knew the deepest, darkest and saddest truth of all: her child was dead.

The mournful wail of the heartbroken mother carried over the campground, across the water and seemed to penetrate every living place and person. It surely penetrated my heart and soul.

I was helpless to bring any healing or hope. Words were empty vessels. Reassurances seemed shallow. I could only stand beside her and accept her sorrow. I could feel tears in my eyes as I realized the enormity of her loss, and thought of my grandson.

The ambulance was nestled behind two big cedar trees which gave a measure of protection for the grieving mother as the news media—ever accurately aware of the subtle changes in the unfolding drama—lined up to record this sad human tragedy. I helped Mom into the ambulance where I was struck by the deep silence that enveloped the tiny space.

The mother sat on the ledge beside the gurney on which lay the body of her little boy. Blankets covered his body, leaving only his head to be seen. His hair was wet and drops of lake water slowly drained from his hair onto the white sheets. A fishing line was still circled around his neck by his left shoulder. He lay forever quiet. Still, he looked as if he were sleeping and would awaken at any moment and be his previous light-hearted, energetic, five-year-old self. I wanted him to wake up.

But now, the whole world was incomprehensible. Carefully, she stroked his hand and said to his unhearing ears, "Oh my baby, my baby. I'm so sorry. I'm so sorry!"

A while later, with Mom under the care of her friends and the ambulance and its precious cargo on its way to the local mortuary, I walked among the rescue workers to offer a last pastoral contact. Quietly, they packaged their equipment. Very few spoke. A few stood alone by themselves and looked silently toward the dock where the memory of this once bright-eyed child seemed still to linger. The western sky was orange but fading moment by moment to a deep darkness just like our spirits.

"I'm OK, Tom," said a diver. "It's just hard when it's a kid."

Oh, yes.

WE'VE GOT A MOTHER TO TELL

We turned south off US 50 onto Ridge Road and drove for several miles. It was quiet. A fall moon hung overhead, giving an eerie pale light to the fields. The bright colors of the countryside were muted and the landscape was like a black and white photograph. Nine-fifteen didn't say much. He never does. If you don't know him you might be put off by his stony silence. But I don't mind. He's not bored or bewildered. He's not disinterested or insensitive, either. He's just private by nature and probably doesn't like making small talk. His best friends know that. It's just the way he is.

He had dispatch call me a half hour earlier. That's easier for me than an unexpected knock on my door in the middle of the night summoning me to a tragedy. It was about 2:00 AM when they called. I was in a deep sleep. I've done this for so long that I can usually answer the phone in the middle of the first ring, but no later than before it rings a second time.

"Tom, this is dispatch. Nine-fifteen asked that you be called. We've had a homicide and he's going to pick you up and go to the parent's home for notification." The call which summons me to my pastoral task is inevitably terse and sketchy with only the bare bones of information at hand. I will have to wait for the rest of the story to unfold on the way to the scene.

I dressed quickly and waited. Those few minutes are like no other in my life. It gives me time to find an emotional and spiritual center where I can think about what it is I am about to do. It's never enough for me just to do the job. I need to think about the event and anticipate what it will be like to tell a parent her child is dead. Not many people have this privilege or bear this responsibility. I may have done it dozens of times in my years as a police chaplain, but that familiarity does not really bring much comfort. Each moment is new. Each event is sad. Each family is different.

Because every moment is unique, I have learned to be prepared for almost any contingency. But of all the death notifications I do, the hardest one is to tell a parent that their son or daughter was murdered. That one didn't die accidentally; there wasn't a silent, undetected medical problem that insidiously stole their life from them. There was no accidental fall from a lethal height or even a heartrending auto accident. These are all sad occasions, but to some degree, people seem able to accept accidents and illnesses as somehow a part of the natural order of human frailty. Unexpected deaths always hurt, but most people find a way to weave such tragedies into the fabric of their lives. But not so with a homicide. It is different when someone has intentionally and wickedly killed your child. Nothing prepares you for that.

Murder leaves parents with unanswered questions and rips their souls to shreds. I hate to break this kind of news to families. How could someone have so despised your son or daughter that they planned and plotted their death? Or was it simply a needless, spontaneous moment of rage, and if so, how could someone have such poor impulse control? And what do you do with all the anger that fills your heart and leaves you without any real resolution?

There are unspoken concerns, too. Was my son secretly involved in something so sinister that he betrayed the wrong people and was killed for his transgression? Or was it simply a matter of my daughter being in the wrong place at the wrong time? And does it make any difference anyway? These death notifications are always complicated because the death was a homicide. Very likely these parents will live forever with unanswered questions and the pain of unrealized hopes. They may wonder if they failed to protect their child when he or she was younger. Or failed to instill the right values. It is a hurt that lasts a lifetime.

I was glad for the quiet time as we drove through the county to the crime scene. I needed to give some thought to the gravity of the work we were about to do. I needed to respect the pain I was about to give to another.

We drove down the tree covered lane to the victim's home. There wasn't much to do at the crime scene, but it always seems important, nevertheless, to take note of the scene itself. It might seem odd that I do this, but it helps me to have been at the setting where the tragedy took place. It is not curiosity; it is my way of experiencing and understanding the extent of the event.

All the deputies and firefighters and paramedics know that I choose to be a witness to the tragedies where they respond. It gives me a firsthand experience with them on the scene, and I can more effectively care for them as well.

I walked across the front lawn to the old farmhouse and stepped inside. One dim light brightened the living room where the paramedics were writing their reports. A deputy was shooting pictures in another room and his flash illuminated the nearly hidden kitchen for a fraction of a second. But mostly it was quiet. Death houses have a quietness that is as cold as winter.

"In here, Tom," spoke a paramedic, startling me.

"Watch where you step," added the other deputy taking pictures.

"There's blood everywhere and we don't want the scene messed up anymore than it already is."

I knew what that meant. This is one persistent tension between rescue workers and cops. The paramedic's first consideration is patient care. Crime scene protection comes next. Cops want that, too, but securing the scene has a valid claim on the moment and they seek to protect it as best they can. But this time the patient was long since dead.

He was the first thing I saw when I entered the kitchen. He was sitting in a chair beside the kitchen table. His arms hung at each side, his hands were open and empty. His legs were extended in front of him. His head tilted backwards behind him. His mouth was wide open. His eyes were open, too, and seemed to look vacantly into the empty room.

Was the assailant someone he knew? Had there been cross words? Did this tragedy take him by surprise? I must have wondered a dozen possibilities as I stood there, captivated by the tragedy. What were his last moments like? Did he have regrets which tormented him? Was he even aware that danger lurked in the shadows of his life and maybe even the shadows of his home? Was he killed by a friend or family member? He had lived life on the edge and may have suffered the consequences of a life lived in a world of drugs and alcohol.

Maybe we would never know.

He wore only a pair of boxer shorts, but they, like his chest and legs, were drenched in blood. A large puddle of thickening blood circled his feet and pooled around the wooden chair. A single, deep gash left a gaping hole right in the center of his chest. On the floor, half in and half out of the pool of blood lay a long, serrated butcher knife. Whoever was responsible for this tragedy had long since left.

The chaplain's work is a silent part of law enforcement. While we may do the one piece that most officers hate to do, death notification, we also may be present on the scene as events unfold. We are a witness to the same gory details, and see its impact on the officers and paramedics. Sometimes we do nothing at all except listen to the stories, validate the hard work done in grim circumstances, and affirm the professionalism of the officers when they work in difficult situations.

"Ready?" asked 915. His voice pulled me out of my thoughts to the task at hand. "He's got a mother we have to tell. Let's get this over with."

DEATH AT MORGAN CROSSING

"Chaplain Shane. This is 911. We need you to respond to the scene of a fatality. It is five miles west of Old 81 at Morgan Crossing. That's where the railroad tracks intersect with the gravel road. We've had a car versus train accident. Two teenagers were involved. One was killed and the other was Life-Watched to Wesley Medical Center. They were both seniors at Jefferson High School."

I cringed as I hung up the phone. I could already guess the sorrow I would encounter. It takes my breath away. Delivering death messages is painful no matter how often you've done them. Each time seems unique and each one is sad. With this one I felt a wave first of relief and then guilt wash over me—Jefferson was a neighboring community, so I was less likely to know the victims and their families and would be spared the personal pain of having to tell such awful news to parents whom I personally knew. Then I felt guilt because, whether I knew them or not, the parents would be utterly devastated, and my relief was only my self-protection.

On the long drive to the deadly intersection, I found myself ruminating about other tragic deaths I have worked and all the other children who have died. Some of these deaths are truly accidents—sad and painful, but without negligence or malice. And some are absolutely preventable. They hurt the most.

I still remember another accident on Old 81, where two children, riding a moped, were run over by a drunk driver who was so intoxicated he was not aware of the accident. Only the grinding of the moped under his car and the screeching noise of the metal as it scraped deep gouges in the concrete made him stop. When I pass that sacred spot, I still see the green Plymouth Fury resting in the southbound lane with its sleek hood all tangled up with the handlebars. I will never dislodge the pitiful wail of the parents of one of the children who happened along the scene quite by accident, and recognized the mangled body of their child. Their howls crossed the prairie like wailing ghosts. No one should know such a moment.

But that was years ago and was only a memory. This is another time and another family.

I parked my truck a hundred yards away and approached the scene. The train was quiet. The engine was several hundred yards away and the long line of freight cars blocked the intersection and snaked a half mile farther back. It takes a long time to bring a freight train to a halt. The train crew huddled together, giving statements to the sheriff's deputies. Their faces looked haggard and weary. They must have died a thousand deaths themselves in that endless moment as they watched the small truck race toward the intersection and disintegrate before their eyes. They will be haunted by this forever, and it wasn't even their fault.

A small Ford Ranger lay in a pile of gravel. Crushed, like some used up soft drink can which had been run over by a tractor trailer rig. The driver's side was simply gone. What remained of the truck was smashed into the passenger's side. It's a wonder and a blessing anyone survived. In fact, the survival of the passenger who barely hung on to his life might not be a blessing at all. Severely injured with multiple broken bones, he also suffered a closed head injury. I wondered if he would recover at all, and if he did, if he might be lost in some confused, twisted world of lingering problems so severe that he would never be the same again. Sometimes death is a friend.

Our job was to travel to another neighboring town to tell a mother that her son had lost his life when he was hit by a train. In a few minutes, this refreshing spring morning would suddenly turn into a horrid nightmare from which one woman would desperately hope to wake up. But she would not be able to free herself from this never-ending nightmare and her unanswered questions. This woman was still filled with grief over the untimely death of the boy's father only eighteen months before. He had died in a freak skiing accident after he crashed head first into a tree. So much grief. So much sadness. So much to accept and try to understand. My heart was heavy. I carried all of this information with me as I left with a deputy and went to her place of employment.

In my experience most deputies don't dwell on the difficult human side of law enforcement when they begin their careers. Mostly, it is the lure of adventure and an abiding sense of justice that entices them. And that's all there. But never far away is the reality that the human element is inevitably and essentially woven into the work. Law enforcement is, fundamentally, a people job. Sometimes it's cops and robbers; but always it is police and people.

Today, a kind and gracious mother must be told an awful truth. And on some occasions, people will hear such news about several members of their family. It's enough to break your heart. And in these times, even cops are touched by the raw edge of life. Certainly the investigation must be managed well, and family members informed properly. But, beyond the facts are the feelings, and we in law enforcement and related fields are at our best when we remember the art of compassion.

WHEN JIMMY RETURNED

Rain fell as a persistent drizzle as I drove with the trooper to the small town where we were to deliver the death message. The gloomy weather seemed providentially appropriate. Dull, gray clouds hovered not far above tree-top level making the late afternoon seem sad. Indeed, both the day and our task was heavy with sorrow. We didn't talk much as we drove along and when we did, it was chit-chat—the kind which keeps your mind off what you have to do—to tell a family that someone they love has died in a highway fatality.

"I hate this part," said the trooper. "I'm glad you're here to do it. I just can't find the words to say. It's one part about this job I don't like." Certainly he was not alone. *No one* likes to give death messages. You feel as if you somehow caused this great sorrow.

We found the address. This tragedy was made worse because the family we were to contact had just had a funeral that very morning for the victim's father. How could any of them know that their grief would soon be compounded when we told them of yet another loss that they must bear? True to custom, family and friends had gathered after the burial to tell stories, eat together, and help each other cope with their pain. And now, we would have to tell the family that the son of the deceased whom they had just buried hours ago was killed in an accident on his way home from his father's funeral. Two family members were dead on the same day. With their grief still raw from one major loss, this family would have to find a way to make room for a second round of sorrow.

I walked through the spring rain, up a rickety staircase to the front porch and felt my anxiety rise. An older woman greeted us at the front door and invited us inside the small house. Little children played on the floor, kept inside because of the weather. The dining room table was full of food brought in by attentive neighbors. Like all grieving homes at such times, there was a blend of reactions from tear-stained faces to smiles as friends who hadn't seen each other for years paid their respects. They told stories, "Remember when …, " to each other. "Please, everybody. Be quiet!" said the matriarch of the clan when we told her we had some important and difficult news to tell them. "The police have something to say," she insisted.

A hush settled around the kitchen table and the trooper said, "The chaplain needs to tell you something, so please listen." With that introduction given, I felt their eyes turn toward me.

"I'm afraid we have more bad news. There's been an accident near Topeka. It involves John. He was in a collision with a truck and we are so sorry to say that he was killed."

With that heart-breaking news now fully known, more grieving began. Some cried openly. Some left the kitchen and sought solace outside, despite the rain. Others held each other. Some looked angrily into space. It just wasn't fair. And it was too much for one family to bear—a father and his son both dead on the same day. They looked stunned.

John's mother put her hands to her face in shock, then composed herself and said, "Oh my word. This is awful. Just awful. It's going to be bad when Jimmy returns. Real bad. He went to buy beer. He took his grandfather's death real hard, and now his dad's gone, too. He's going to be angry!"

Presently I heard the unmistakable sound of a big Harley rumbling up the driveway. Jimmy had returned. It was quiet in the kitchen. Everyone stepped aside to give Jimmy room when he appeared. No one wanted to be nearby when he was told of this new development. They seemed to know what would happen. Seeing the trooper standing by the table, he tossed the beer down and demanded, "What's wrong! Why are you here?"

It was the sound of pent-up grief. I've heard it before. I've felt it myself when my own dad died. It's all the hurt that a person feels that has been contained inside and never released, that now was beginning to erupt. There was no delaying the inevitable and no need to ease into this tragedy, so I said to him, "Jimmy, I'm Chaplain Shane. This is Trooper Price. We have some difficult news to tell you. There has been a wreck. It involves your dad. We are very sorry to have to tell you that he was killed on his way home from your grandfather's funeral."

Rarely have I seen such anger and rage consume someone so suddenly. "The hell you say!" said the enraged Jimmy. Then as if I had assaulted him, he glared at me, doubled both his fists, and drew his right fist back ready to strike me. His faced flushed as he glared at me, the bearer of the bad message, and I stood ready for what I felt would be an altercation.

Quietly, deftly but with conviction, the trooper stepped ever so slightly between us and said, "We're terribly sorry, Jimmy. We can only tell you that for reasons we may never know, there was a head-on collision and your father was killed."

The enraged Jimmy turned aside and slammed his doubled-up fist into the wall, instead of me, smashing it directly into a stud. He winced in pain as his injured hand matched his own injured and broken spirit. His beloved grandfather and his dad were dead on the same day. This man hurt as deeply inside himself as he possibly could.

Grief is a strange experience. It has a way of lurking inside your soul and coming out in twisted ways. We did our best to bring this awful reality to light with grace and compassion. But some news is too unbearable to hear with sensibility. To some few, it results in pent-up rage as was the case with Jimmy. Most notifications leave people wounded, but accepting. Their anger is rarely directed toward law enforcement.

Death messages are hard to do as they remind us of the fragility of existence and how all of us live at the edge of life.

DEATH ON DUTCH AVENUE

"Six-o-six, need you to respond to a fatality accident. We have three fatals and three injured. Two were flown to Wesley Medical Center. One was taken to Moundridge Hospital."

I hung up the phone and left the hospital where I work. Care for the critically injured is what I do for a living. It's the nature of hospital chaplaincy. I take my turn as the on-call chaplain, and am regularly summoned to the Emergency Department where a team of highly trained medical and surgical specialists work intensely to push back the onslaught of death and destruction. The best minds, the most skilled technicians, the latest equipment—all are brought to bear to bring hope and healing to strangers who, in a devastating moment in time, tumble to the brink of life itself and often hover for minutes or hours … or longer … in a twilight zone where either life or death may be the final outcome. And for a while, no one is sure what that outcome will be.

I sped north on I-135 past Newton, where I live, then seven more miles to Hesston, where I turned west on Dutch Avenue. It had been dusk when I left, but night had settled on the prairie when I reached the scene itself. I like working with technicians at the hospital and take comfort in knowing that these surgeons are highly skilled, and that they have learned how to touch the sacred essence of life. But my work has nothing to do with the skill of technology. We chaplains work with no sophisticated equipment. We enter the center of these crises with only ourselves, and our task is to try as best we can to make sense out of the senseless. If technicians deal with body systems, chaplains are concerned with people, their faith, and their spirits.

Once at the scene, I parked my truck and walked past the deputy who stood in the darkness beside his patrol unit. We signaled a greeting to one another and I walked on.

I stopped briefly on the bridge to peer into the smashed car— a twisted mass of steel and plastic, its roof had ripped off like an open can of vegetables. The seriously injured passengers, a mother and daughter, had been removed, but I could see how their memories littered the empty car. A tiny doll lay on the floor. School books lay open and pages fluttered in the early winter breeze. A white sweater sat empty in the front seat, stained crimson from blood. A bag of groceries with an assortment of cans and frozen goods was scattered on the back seat. At the edge of the bridge and down a steep embankment lay the other car. The sheriff greeted me and we talked casually for a moment, trying to keep a slight distance from the horror of events like these.

As I crept down the steep embankment with the sheriff, brilliant spotlights from the rescue trucks illuminated the tragedy. The roar of the generator was deafening. We had to talk loudly to hear.

I stepped close to the vehicle. Still strapped inside the car were three Code Black occupants. One additional passenger, seriously injured, had already been rushed to the hospital. "Code Black" is another way we keep our safe distance from the reality of death. We don't name it. At my hospital, no one "dies." We say, "Respirations Have Ceased (RHC)." We do a lot to keep the truth out of immediate awareness. But here that was not possible. Right before me were three people who, just an hour ago, were on their way somewhere.

"This is really sad. They are all Holdermans," the sheriff said to me. "The deputy needs you to go with him to Moundridge to meet with the families." Indeed, in the bright light of the rescue units' spotlights, the faith tradition of the occupants was obvious by their dress.

Those in the Holderman faith, a branch of the Mennonite tradition, have more strict guidelines to behavior than most other people follow. The men wear beards. The women wear black bonnets. You can't find a more simple and honest group than these. They work hard. They are self-sufficient. And they are decent people.

When I arrived at the small town hospital, the church community was already gathering. Word had spread. Families came. The women all wore plain print dresses with black shoes. The men were dressed in trousers and white shirts. They stood silently. Already they knew that four people from their church were in an accident.

The sheriff's deputy, Jimmy, spoke first, giving the details of the incident, at least as much as was known. It was hard to tell the silent group of believers that three of their community had died in a collision on a quiet country road not so far from where they lived.

I shook their hands, one by one. Their deeply-held faith seemed to be the comfort that sustained them. That and the closeness of their community. A great quietness had settled over the room. They held each other and looked sadly at the floor. Confronted with a truth that seemed too hard to hear and too difficult to believe, somehow the brutal reality of the news was wrapped around the world of faith as symbolized by the presence of the chaplain. After a while we said our goodbyes as gently as possible, and Jimmy and I quietly left the hospital. We drove away in silence, feeling the sorrow of the group.

The Chaplain's Notebook
Part III: Death Notification: Principles and Procedures

There can be no preparation or rehearsal for something like death notification. But, out of the sadness of each one of those encounters I've been part of over the years, I've tried to develop some guidelines about what must happen.

1. The sad news of death must be brought with love and care. It will wound deeply, so the way the news is conveyed is very important. It ought never to be done with the cold precision of an obligatory task.

2. People need to know what happened. Tell them what facts are known. Keep things simple. Even though grief makes it hard to remember, hearing the information helps make it real. We may never know the "why" of such moments, but we can share the details of the event, the sequence of what happened, those involved, and the results.

3. There are lots of procedural questions that must be answered and often the chaplain or the trooper can help. They may wonder: Was he in pain? Where is the body? What are the legal implications of this event? Where is the car? What happened to his belongings? How do I get the body back here? Chaplains are not expected to know all these answers, but they can be helpful in connecting the bereaved with the proper authorities who will be able to find the answers.

4. The chaplain's task, in a sense, is to try to humanize a broken moment in time. We seek to try to help people move beyond their bewilderment to some measure of stability. This is a crucial time to rally their natural caregivers to their side—family, neighbors, church members, pastor, priest, rabbi, friends—all of whom may be helpful to them. We must respect their wish to be by themselves, but it does not hurt to gently press the offer to make a few phone calls, and to stay until support comes.

5. Anger, tears, and questions are all a part of the grief process. It is uncomfortable to stand in the presence of such sorrow, but encouragement to "be strong" is not as healing or as helpful as allowing a genuine experience of sadness.

6. Frequently, an explicit faith response is useful. Some want and need to pray. Some ask why. Some feel the absence of God and blame God for their sorrow. When that happens we may wish they had more faith, but we can respect the truth that their faith response is authentic for them. And some are comforted by a very traditional faith support. We begin where the bereaved are, theologically and emotionally.

***

There are a number of tasks that chaplains can offer. Besides understanding, and in addition to the gift of a pastoral presence, there are specific things that can be very helpful.

1. Chaplains can accept the burden of bringing the bitter news of a tragedy with as much love and gentle caring as is possible. Chaplains generally have some level of relationship with local clergy, and when such relationships exist between victims and a church, chaplains can expedite the caring process this faith community can offer.

2. Chaplains are able to help with the early integration of facts and feelings. Knowing the facts helps with the healing process. Even if many details get lost in the fog of grief, still the presented

reality is truth and must be reckoned with. As difficult as it is to hear that a loved one committed suicide, it is a reality that must be addressed.

3. Chaplains can help handle the details surrounding a sudden death. The family will have questions about the funeral, whether there might be an autopsy, the need to identify the body, or the location of the deceased's belongings.

4. In the whirl of procedures that emergencies bring, the tasks often crowd out the human drama. The bewilderment of a crisis is paralyzing. Helping to facilitate a healthy expression of grief is useful. Until such time as natural care givers can be brought to the moment, the presence of a chaplain can be redemptive. The matter of being willing to be fully present with another has its own claim. This includes both victims and caregivers.

5. So often in such crisis moments, people feel nearly shattered and the incident exposes their strengths and weaknesses. In these devastating times, the bedrock themes of faith are laid bare. Now is not the time for easy faith answers which are sometimes offered as quick fixes to bind wounds or ease pain. Instead, it is the time to accept the wonder, share the hurt, and both represent and re-present the presence of a caring God. Some are angry at God. Some want and need to pray. Some benefit from the gathering of their church members. Some have no faith background or church members.

6. Victims and survivors are the first ones clergy attend to in a crisis, but care must be given to those heroic men and women who work the traumas: the paramedics, the firefighters, and those in law enforcement. When the energy of the event settles down, their own feelings surface and must be attended to.

X
CHAPLAINCY AND TERRORISM

The on-duty chaplain was summoned to an in-coming Life Watch helicopter transfer from western Kansas. A three-year-old child was gravely sick with an unknown illness and was being flown to Wesley Medical Center for intensive care. His mother accompanied him. Because I was assigned to the Pediatric Intensive Care Unit, I was instructed to meet her there.

I stood with Dr. Pickert, the pediatrician, just inside the PICU doors as the infant and his terrified mother entered. The young mother looked to be about eighteen. Her body shook from fear and she stared blankly at us. I had been told that she had only a minimal understanding of English.

Dr. Pickert tried as best he could to help her understand that he and his team of physicians and nurses would evaluate the nature of her baby's illness, determine the gravity of his condition and begin to treat him. He promised to update her on her child's status as soon as he had fresh information to share. She nodded in agreement, probably trusting in his expertise and certainly his kindness.

"I want you to go with Chaplain Shane," Dr. Pickert directed her. "He'll take you to a family waiting room and be with you. I'll come out as soon as possible to give you a report. Then we will get you back with your child as soon as we can." Her eyes glistened with tears which she blinked back, trying hard to focus. She nodded her head as if understanding.

I did take her back to the family room where we would wait together for the doctor's status report. This mostly bare and unfriendly room would eventually be remodeled into a pleasant, warm, and inviting place for families. But today, two old couches lined the walls, facing a television set. A game show was on TV, but the young mother paid no attention. Sometimes she looked at me and smiled a weak "thank you" but mostly she held her hands close to her face and rocked back and forth.

It was April 19, 1995, and my wife's birthday. It was supposed to be a special day for us. Suddenly, the television game show was interrupted by a network announcer. "This just in from Oklahoma City. The Murrah Federal Building has been shattered by a blast of unknown origin. We don't yet know the number of casualties or injuries, but it is presumed the toll will be high. We also know there was a daycare center somewhere in the building."

Live television pictures from a circling helicopter showed the billowing smoke rising from the disaster. A massive pile of rubble stood in the ruins where a government building had once been. The scene was at once threatening and compelling. The report continued with more live pictures, and from everywhere in the room, even families with very sick children watched the unfolding horror. The more it became certain that the daycare center was buried under the mound of rubble, the more distressed all of us became.

Then came the most unsettling news—it appeared to be a disaster caused by human hands! I was working in a medical unit dedicated to the healing of children. This was our passion and we were there by choice. And now, every television in the PICU showed those early pictures of the shattered building and the pile of rubble under which the daycare children were buried.

Another chaplain colleague, Carol Meredith, alerted me that Wesley Medical Center was placed on stand-by, potentially expecting to receive patients from our sister HCA (Hospital Corporation of America) facility in Oklahoma City. A sense of urgency swept through our hospital as we watched the developing tragedy in this city, which is only 157 miles from Witchita

An on-call chaplain came to be with the young mother as she waited for word on the care of her baby, and I never did learn whether he survived to become a football player, or an honor student, or both, in some high school in western Kansas. I went to lunch, but returned early, wanting to be ready for the possible arrival of trauma patients. Our students were alerted and began preparing to work a major catastrophe.

When I walked into the pastoral care office, Dr. James Stapleford, our director, notified me that the hospital was sending a team down to Oklahoma City to assist with this disaster. "I want you and Carol to get ready to go with the Wesley group to work with Presbyterian Medical Center," he said.

And so began my first week-long critical incident pastoral care intervention. I know it helped to have had twenty years experience as a police chaplain. It helped to have had experience in our own hospital working traumas. And it helped to be a CISM (Critical Incident Stress Management) trainer. But past experience aside, the actual on-scene work proved to be staggering. During my time there I was stunned; I was saddened; I was often angry. But I was also ready and willing to stay. To me, it seemed the fulfillment of a lifetime of preparation. God had prepared me to be here, both personally and professionally.

This tragedy, like national disasters, requires medical care, nursing care, and mental health care. But there is also a need for spiritual care. Not every pastor is prepared for or has an interest in such work anymore than every physician is prepared to perform surgery. But for those who are so equipped, the spiritual needs in a disaster are raw and messy and the need for spiritual care is urgent.

I think of disaster care as a "Theology for the Empty Spaces of Life." The church has long made the claim that everyone, sinners and saints alike, are welcome. We have repeatedly said that, in the community of faith, one can find hope and healing. But there are times in life when some people are too broken, too fearful, and too shattered to come through the church's open doors for the hope and help they need. The church needs to go to them and this means going into the shadows of life, the broken places where there is intense suffering, and where evil seems more present than kindness, and where God seems hidden. When terrorism has temporarily cast the world into darkness, the Church needs to take its small light of hope and kindness to those broken in body and soul.

The stories that follow speak of some of the times and ways some of us have sought to walk into the darkness with the Good News.

THE MURRAH BUILDING

I passed through the first security check station and showed my badge. That was all I had needed to do the day before—show the clear plastic card with my name and the agency I was with to the security guard. But, only twenty-four hours later the security here had tightened up considerably. We all had to face the truth that our freedom comes at a cost. The opportunity to come and go as we pleased, and to speak our minds as we wanted, had been rescinded, and all our privileges were being cautiously reviewed.

"Sir, I'll need to see a second picture ID. No offense intended. We are requiring this of everyone," said the young National Guardsman. Other military personnel stood nearby along with representatives from the local Sheriff's Department. Everyone was polite, even mildly apologetic. But firm. They looked carefully at me to see if I appeared other than who I claimed to be.

Soon I was allowed through. The first perimeter, that is. It was the same story when I approached the second tier of armed guards in front of the command center, only this time the number of guards was increased manyfold. More protection. More caution. I wondered what it would be like in other countries where such security is the norm.

But this was no normal time. This tragedy was willfully inflicted on unsuspecting and undeserving people by those who apparently believed that terror was the way to bring about the changes they thought were necessary. Their point appeared buried under the rubble, along with the children who began their day in innocence and moments later turned their laughter into screams. Such utter disregard for life prompted this unprecedented security concern.

The third tier of security was closest to the Murrah Federal Building itself. Having negotiated my way this far did not make the third gate any easier to pass.

"I'll need to see another picture ID," said the armed officer.

Together with other chaplains who worked this critical event I had a twofold task. When we were "on scene" we walked around the edge of the disaster area offering support to individual rescue workers. We went to the rescue worker respite centers, offering support. And at the hospital we did group support, allowing hospital staff an opportunity to talk about their experiences.

I remember an unknown nurse who wept as she said to me the day before, "I'm afraid to go anywhere. I can't even go to church because what if they blow that up too?"

Another person said, "I'm afraid to go into tall buildings and now I can't go into basements either because that's where so many people were crushed." Nothing seemed secure anymore.

After a disaster of this magnitude we all needed to find a new normal. We needed to grieve the senseless deaths of those sweet children and unsuspecting adults. In our heart of hearts, we knew (and feared) that it could have been any of us.

We had to fashion a new faith in all our ordinary lives and in everyday moments. It was time for us to open our hearts, renew our faith, and rebuild again in the spirit of all those who had walked through and beyond their tragedies towards hope.

NEW YORK CITY

I climbed onto the Gator parked in front of the temporary morgue and began the short journey through the debris field to the "Pit" itself. Once known as the "Pile," it was now a deepening hole formed as firefighters and steelworkers relentlessly removed the tangled mass of steel, concrete, cables, and pipes from the collapsed Twin Towers of the World Trade Center. It was mid-November, but the weather was still warm. I looked through the chain link fence a couple hundred yards away to the dust-filled, debris-strewn empty space where I was soon to be driven. It was Ground Zero, and I had been summoned because another MOS had just been found.

MOS means "Member of Service." An ironworker, uncovering a tangled jumble of debris, had found the partial remains of a

163

firefighter, so identified by the decaying heavy coat and Scott pack still strapped to his back. When an MOS was found everything came to a standstill, the body was extricated, a chaplain offered a blessing, and the body was brought to the temporary morgue for an initial documentation. This simple ritual was followed hundreds of times as a way to honor those who died following this worst ever attack on American soil.

For two weeks in November 2001 I was serving in New York City. My assignment as a volunteer was the temporary morgue (TMOR) at Ground Zero. Just a few hundred yards from the Pit itself, the TMOR was a hastily assembled wooden building planted at the base of the towering NASDAQ building. This fifty-story glass and steel structure, by any other standard, was an awesome sight, yet for years it had been dwarfed by the gigantic Twin Towers. Now there was nothing left but a gaping hole and a dwindling pile of debris where the towers once stood. I was assigned to the temporary morgue when it was learned that I had prior experience with local law enforcement. The morgue was largely staffed by the NYPD, Port Authority Police Department (PAPD), and the New York State Police officers, and it was correctly understood that the chaplain assigned to the morgue ought to be someone who both understood and valued the law enforcement culture. I was honored to accept this assignment, though most of my friends were aghast that I did. The very thought of the morgue conjures up gruesome images, but the reality was that it was a setting of great reverence, respect, and dedicated work.

I sat on the Gator, that small four-wheeled vehicle favored by hunters and ranchers, as we navigated our way through the muddy acres of Ground Zero, finally coming to a stop at the base of the deep pit. I stepped off the Gator and reported to the fire captain.

"Stand by, Chaplain, it'll be a few minutes. They're still down there. You can see them. They're getting the body loaded and the flag on. We'll call you when we're ready."

That moment's pause allowed me to look around. I stood in the middle of Ground Zero. It was dirty and the air was pungent with a foul haze that smelled rancid. My eyes burned. I kept the breathing apparatus snugly on my face since I didn't want to breathe in any more of the poisonous air than I had to.

Standing at the Pit, I was suddenly aware of how quiet it had become. All around me gigantic cranes, bulldozers, and other huge machines with claw-like hands, normally used to pick up tons of debris, were resting silently. No one spoke. A gentle stillness settled over the place. Firefighters slowly fell into two lines leading up from the Pit to an awaiting ambulance. An honor guard of firefighters—but instead of the crisp, pressed dress uniforms of most honor guards, they wore their dirty gear. That seemed right.

The small assemblage of firefighters deep in the Pit first placed a red biohazard bag inside a black body bag, zipped it shut, then gently placed it on a stretcher. Over that, an American flag was respectfully draped. Then the six firefighters, walking as pallbearers, cautiously brought the MOS up a concrete and rubble strewn path.

A New York steelworker stood beside me. He leaned on an iron pole and together we watched the ascent. He was big. His features were rugged. His face was smudged by hours of working. A look of intense determination marked his face. Quietly, together, we waited for the body to be brought up. Then he touched my arm and said, "Thanks for being here, Chaplain." He didn't speak for a while longer, then asked, "Who takes care of *you*?"

I was caught off guard by his kindness. Indeed, I had wanted this assignment of caring for both the dead and the workers, and was not expecting anything in return. Plenty of care was available to me from other volunteers who were working at the scene, and from my family whom I called daily. Still, his question was an act of kindness, and my spirit was touched by his outreach.

All too soon, the captain yelled, "Chaplain!" and I moved to the edge of the Pit at the head of the double line of firefighters.

"Uncover!" ordered the captain. With that order given, all helmets came off. The captain then nodded to me. I stood at the head of the stretcher and offered a prayer and a blessing.

In the center of that wretched place full of dirt and rage and sorrow, right there where two hundred firefighters stood in reverent attention and hundreds of other steel workers watched silently, I had a profound sense that I was standing on holy ground. Certainly it lacked the grace and beauty of a cathedral—this mound of debris, littered with artifacts from the Twin Towers and the invisible remains of thousands of lives of innocent victims of this tragedy. But I had a profound sense that God was present in every piece of concrete slab, every scoop full of debris lifted and removed, and the aluminum facade still protruding from the ground. My understanding of holy or sacred ground was forever changed.

In three decades of ministry, I had never experienced such respect or support for faith, nor such openness to the symbols of faith—prayer and blessings. People experienced a hunger for some word of comfort beyond that which they could give themselves.

With my blessing complete, I walked slowly up the steep incline to the waiting ambulance. Once there, the doors were opened and the remains of the MOS were placed inside. I entered the back of the ambulance and sat on the bench beside the body. It was quiet inside the ambulance. Outside, the machines began to dig again. The firefighters resumed their recovery work. I waited for the driver to take us back to the TMOR. In the meantime, I listened to the quiet. I experienced this as a holy responsibility and a privilege.

This work, this vigil, did not seem gruesome or odd. It seemed like an honor. It was an opportunity to accompany not just the fragments of a body, but the dreams of a family. Here was a father, a brother, a mother, or even a sister for all I knew. I was with someone who once shared dreams with other people; dreams that would never come to pass. Was there a son, perhaps, who went fly fishing in the Rockies with him just as I go with my son? I hoped there were enough memories to sustain his loved ones for the empty days that would surely come. I hoped they could draw strength from the realization that this beloved person gave his life in service for others.

Back at the TMOR, I stepped outside the ambulance as a dozen NYPD stood at attention and honored this recovered victim as he was removed. I opened the door of the tiny frame building, then stepped inside and held it open as the firefighters carried their burden past a cluttered desk filled with report forms and old coffee cups, stepped around an equipment table and a shelf filled with medical equipment and laid the black plastic body bag onto the gleaming, stainless steel examining table. Since this was two months past the catastrophe itself, by now, mostly only fragments were found.

The Medical Examiner stood at the side of the table. He was authoritative. A scowl crossed his face when he discovered the body fragment was not accompanied by the right documentation. He erupted in a stream of angry admonitions about how *"absolutely essential"* such GPS and descriptive documentation was so they could "account for the *exact* location of this victim" in the World Trade Center when the determination of his identity was made. He concluded his tirade with a lengthy string of expletives, when his eyes suddenly locked onto me. He looked stunned and somewhat embarrassed.

When I first arrived in New York City two weeks before Thanksgiving in the aftermath of the 9/11 catastrophe, I was asked by the team leader about my work history. Since I was a chaplain in a level 1 trauma center, a CISM trainer, and had been a police chaplain and reserve officer for nearly a quarter century, he decided he needed me to work at the morgue. "You're used to trauma, and that is one place where you'll work closest with cops. I need someone who understands that culture and can fit in," he said. He was right. I did know this culture.

"Oh, I'm so sorry, Father," the examiner said immediately. "I didn't mean to offend." With that he returned to his task. He examined the bone and determined it to be a femur and that it was wrapped in a yellow fire coat. Therefore, the victim was likely an MOS. A firefighter. With his apology offered and his examination complete, he nodded to me. It was my turn. I stepped to the side of the examining table, took off my helmet, and said, "Let us pray."

The solemn assembly of yellow-coated firefighters and uniformed officers each took off their head gear and bowed their heads as I said a prayer. With that done, I walked ahead of the body bag through the NYPD honor guard to the waiting ambulance where the MOS was taken to Belleview and the permanent morgue for DNA study.

Seasoned firefighters and law enforcement officers all seemed touched by the simple prayers and the pastoral presence offered by the chaplain. I was granted the privilege of presence in places otherwise off limits. I was able to speak to and listen to officers in moments of emotional distress because the office of chaplain was respected.

I knew I was in New York because nearly everyone called me "Father."

"Are you a Father or a Reverend?" a police officer asked me one day.

"Actually, I'm a Reverend," I responded with a smile.

"I just wanted to make sure. Take care, Father," he said with respect.

After a few days the crusty Medical Examiner had actually befriended me enough to counsel me on self-care lest the toxic dust from the WTC demolition exacerbate my asthma. And if it does, "Call me day or night and we'll take care of you." I knew he meant it.

A BIT OF HOME

Disasters are odd experiences. They are filled with moments of frenzy and times of boredom. My days at Ground Zero were like that. I had lots of time to chat with the New York State Troopers. In fact, it was their job to drive me back to my hotel each evening and that afforded us time to talk.

I took the subway to my assignment each morning, but in the evening, I was told to let them take me home. That was hard to do. I believed if I got myself to work each day, I could just as easily get myself back to the hotel. I knew they had other tasks to do besides escorting me. Soon enough, though, I discovered that I had miscalculated the hospitality of the New York State Troopers. They are an excellent, professional department. When they learned that "back home" I was not only a police chaplain but a reserve officer, they treated me with collegiality and respect.

It never took long before a personal relationship was formed. To find common ground among strangers is not hard in a crisis situation.

"Have you lived all your life in New York?" I asked an officer named Tommy one afternoon.

"For the most part," he responded, then added, "all except for a few years way out west."

My curiosity was hooked, so I pursued his story in more detail. "Out west? Where?" I asked.

"Oh, just a little town in Kansas. You probably never heard of it."

"Really," I said with heightened curiosity. "What town's that? I'm from Kansas."

"I was in a little place called McPherson," he said giving a long "E" sound to his pronunciation.

"McPherson!" I exclaimed. "That's just thirty miles from my home. I live in Newton."

"No kidding," he said almost disbelieving. "I played ball for McPherson College and one of our games was at Bethel College in Newton."

We had discovered an instant point of connection. Then, as if to test the waters even further, he drew near to me, lowered his voice as if telling me something confidential and said, "You ever hear of a place called Kirby's in Wichita?"

"Kirby's?" I said. "You mean the little tavern near Wichita State University? *That* Kirby's?"

Providentially, a couple of NYPD friends of his were walking by when my newfound friend Tommy from the NYPD said, "Hey guys! Father here knows where I used to drink beer in Wichita!"

By any account this was an insignificant moment. Except that in the middle of great sorrow, two strangers met and, for a moment in time, there was community. I was taken in by these officers and made to feel welcome. The friendship of the NYPD, the hospitality of the state troopers, and the respect offered by the FDNY was a point of sweet humanity in an otherwise inhumane time.

CAN'T GO THERE, PADRE.

"Can't go there, Padre. All locked up," said the tough-looking man walking toward me. If I ever stood next to a living example of a Hollywood stereotype, it was now. He looked like a New York City iron worker because he was one. Underneath his hard hat, his red, white, and blue bandanna fluttered in the wind. He was a blue-collar ironworker, solidly union, a red-blooded American and proud of it.

"Every day they change things," he said with mock disgust and a wry smile. "Gotta find a new way around every day," he continued.

I introduced myself and thanked him for his hospitality about directions. We walked down a muddy side street one block off Ground Zero and tried to find the opening to the Red Cross Respite Center at the Marriott Hotel for breakfast.

His white hard hat was covered with stickers: an American flag on one side and an assortment of other symbols on the other. His blue-jean coveralls were smudged with mud. His lean, hard face had rings underneath his eyes where protective glasses kept his eyes more or less clean, but the rest of his face was caked with soot. He looked like a raccoon. His beard stubble gave him a gruff appearance. When we shook hands, I could feel the strength of his grip and the hardness of his fingers.

"How are you doing?" I asked, trying to see if he would share anything more personal than directions. The image of ironworkers is that they are no nonsense, gruff people. That's often true. Every morning as I rode the subway to work I was belly to belly and shoulder to shoulder with strangers. But headsets and newspapers keep people unto themselves. It is a city of distance and strangers. Yet when the greatest tragedy to happen on American soil since the Civil War occurred, New Yorkers opened their hearts and offered incredibly compassionate care.

One day I stepped over a man sleeping on the sidewalk at the subway entrance. He had spread out a *New York Times* to sleep on and covered himself with his coat, then fell asleep. I, of course, was fresh from the Park Central Hotel where I was warm and where my sheets were crisp and clean. I had a hot shower, too. I wonder if he remembered his last hot shower. New York is a city of contrasts and conflicts.

The ironworker continued, "Lady from Connecticut—a newspaper reporter—stopped me yesterday. She asked me how I was doing. I think she was looking for a story, but she was nice. I think she cared. I told her I was OK. We got people like you who ask us how we're doing. It helps. Gives us someone to talk to. It's not easy, you know. We're pulling out our own people here."

"Thanks," I responded, and then added, "I didn't mean to pry where I don't belong. I just wanted to see how you were."

"No, no!' You're not prying," the ironworker reassured me. "It helps."

Everyone said, "Thanks for being here." Deeper than their busy—even gruff—exterior, New Yorkers are as kind as anyone else. Tragedies build communities among strangers. One morning I walked by two cops warming themselves by a blazing fire in a wire basket and we passed the time with casual conversation. "It helps when you people come to help us," said the big cop. "We appreciate it." I thanked him.

Volunteers from many disciplines came to New York City to offer assistance. I was only one of thousands. More than I ever expected, people were willing to accept pastoral care. Somewhere deep inside them, even the strongest among them struggled with questions of faith and meaning. How could such a horrid thing have happened? Why did so many good people suffer and die? Where do we turn for hope? It was a chaplain's task and privilege to listen and offer help.

Each day I made my way out of the Respite Center and returned to my assignment at the morgue. I could not go directly there, though. The way was blocked with police check-points and massive construction trucks carrying debris from Ground Zero to the landfill. I had to slip my way through the side streets and alleys and along back ways to get where I needed to go.

Walking along the streets, I noted the walls of the buildings. What a story they told. In bright day-glow orange spray paint, rescue workers had hastily drawn signs on the walls in the hours after the tragedy giving the terrified citizens directions for where to go: FIRST AID CENTER ... MORGUE, ONE BLOCK ... TRIAGE ... EVACUATE.

Once this was a neighborhood of businesses, small cafés, a Burger King, a financial center, but in a blinking moment of horror these became casualties too. People fled in terror and what once was a thriving Manhattan business center had become an abandoned neighborhood overnight. Every evening at six, my day's work was done, a different state trooper drove me home. "All the way from Kansas," said one. "That's a long way. Thanks."

The destruction at Ground Zero was painful to see and threatening to experience. But rising out of our anguish and anger was our compassion and community. It may have been the worst we have experienced, but it brought out the best that we are.

The Chaplain's Notebook
Part IV: Working in Disaster Situations

Trauma work is exhilarating. The adrenalin rush is energizing. It helps you face incredible tragedy and keep going. It can also cloud your judgment and lead to tragic mistakes. It is easy to be seduced into a Superman mind-set where one begins to believe he can and must work beyond reason and experience.

Following my work in New York City after 9/11, I developed some guidelines which aren't uniquely mine but are a compilation of wise ideas from random sources. No doubt other responders have their own list which would include many of these same ideas. I hope they are useful thoughts to follow about pacing yourself and avoiding the worst consequences of critical incident stress.

1. Have a faith and philosophy which gives you some way to respond to the reality of tragedy and ways to find your own hope and healing. In times of great tragedy, everyone struggles with the problem of evil and why good people suffer. It confronts us when a single child is struck and killed by a drunk driver. But the stakes are even more severe when the casualties are massive and the victims are innocent, as in Oklahoma City or the sites of the September 11, 2001 terrorism. The idea of thousands of deaths stuns us with the unfairness of it all and we hunger for answers.

Being grounded in a faith which gives one hope in trying times is useful for everyone, but for clergy it seems imperative because clergy are expected to be leaders of other helpers and victims alike. When innocent people suffer from natural disasters the question is painful enough. But when the suffering is caused by other humans and the innocent are seen only as "collateral damage," then the problem is exacerbated.

There are no easy answers to the problem of suffering and simplistic answers are not helpful. But somewhere in the mixture of suffering and faith, there are enough places to find a foothold, enough solid ground to give one a place from which to respond without trivializing the suffering or promising easy answers.

Something as seemingly simple as pastoral presence, or believing that God is with us in the depth of our sorrow, may be enough. Or we may believe that God can bring hope even when there seems to be none, or that God is present whenever one person cares for another.

2. Take care of yourself physically. Take your medications. Pace yourself. It seems to be only common sense to take care of yourself this way. Only a fool would ignore his or her self-care. But it happens. The excitement of the tragedy and the unexpected adrenalin rush that comes with it can easily cause us to lose perspective and overlook our own self care. It is too easy to care more for others than to care for ourselves.

But it is wise to remember that self care is the first rule of therapeutic help. If the helper does not take care of him- or herself, sooner than later, the helper will crash and burn and be of no help to the victims of the tragedy. Taking care of one's self is not being selfish; it is good stewardship.

Since I was thirty years of age, I have been a runner. It is my way of keeping myself physically fit and it helps dissipate the intense feelings that build up when working tragedies. It also gives me a half hour to be by myself and to meditate. I made time to run in Oklahoma City and New York City. Some workers came to the tragedy without their medications and had to avail themselves of the physicians on site to supply them. It is always helpful to have appropriate medical care available for rescue workers, but each one of us must be responsible for our own medical, emotional, and spiritual care.

Because crisis work is intense and entails enormous pressure to work effectively and quickly to facilitate search and rescue for helpless victims, it often comes at the cost of healthy self care. This is often seen in the diet of rescue workers, cops and paramedics alike. Chaplains are also caught up in this sense of urgency and the temptation to exist on snacks and fast food.

Disaster work must be done expeditiously and this often translates into food needing to be taken quickly. It is often fast food in every imaginable type. But eating "comfort food," especially snacks and candy bars, is not helpful.

Taking time to eat well, to take a break and replenish oneself … nutritionally, socially, and spiritually … pays dividends. At the World Trade Center, the rescue workers were fed at the Marriott by the American Red Cross and others, so that workers had time away from the tragedy to eat well-prepared food and to disengage from their stressful work for a period of respite

Because bottled water is so readily available there seems no excuse to not stay hydrated. But in the excitement of the crisis work it is easy to overlook this basic human need.

3. Maintain your relationships at home and at the disaster site itself. Don't isolate yourself. Develop connections with colleagues with whom you work or make use of existing relationships if they are already in place. This is no time for a Lone Ranger approach.

Sometimes we are summoned to tragedies far away from our homes and our support systems. It may be that you don't know anyone there and if that is so, it is important that you reach out to others and put something in place.

I knew no one in New York City at the time I was there, so it was essential that I reached out to the other workers. We went to dinner each night after our long day's work. We talked about the events we'd been through. We developed a community. We shared similar experiences and we understood something of each other's lives. My wife's friend Marty also offered to have me meet a friend of hers who happened to be in Manhattan at the time and we got together for a very good evening. In Oklahoma City, a dozen hospital staff from Wesley Medical Center went to help and we had each other for support.

4. Don't be a hero. An often overlooked seduction of trauma work is the reputation we develop for being strong. Sometimes we are labeled as experts in crisis care. Disaster work is not for everyone. Not every physician is suited to be a trauma surgeon, either. Some physicians are better suited for Family Practice medicine. So is it comparably true for clergy. Some are better suited to serve a local parish, work with youth, teach at a university or seminary. Other clergy have the training and the temperament to work disasters. Both are important.

But even the most competent disaster clergy are vulnerable to either traumatic stress or cumulative stress and, when that happens, we need a means to address our own related struggles. It helps us to pace ourselves and not place unrealistic expectations on ourselves. We are part of a team. It is not our sole responsibility to save everyone. The better we learn this, the healthier we will be.

5. Give support to your peers. Those who work in crisis care tend to be a close knit community. The shared risks bond them to one another. Their lives depend on teamwork. Even if they are individually competent they know how much they depend on each other. They also learn that at any given moment they may be called on to offer extra support to a colleague.

I think of this as the "Bucket Theory." All of us carry personal and professional stresses with us all of the time. It is what it means to be human. When our buckets are empty of stress, we have plenty of room to accept either a lot of little stresses or even the ravages of a major event. We can still function well because we have room in our "buckets" and we are not over-burdened.

All of us are vulnerable to discovering that our buckets are full. Perhaps, almost without our awareness, we have experienced an accumulation of stressful events and we have no room for any more.

Our buckets are full. Our resources are depleted. Perhaps the event itself is of such magnitude it overloads our buckets and we have no ability to respond effectively.

Peers generally know one another well enough to discern when a colleague is so burdened that she or he is not functioning well. It is imperative for peers to look out for each other.

6. Stay connected to your family and support system at home. It may be that you are called on to work a tragedy in your own home community. If so, you are geographically close to a loving, supportive community. But even in such an event, you may be cut off from ready access to loved ones due to the demands of the tragedy itself.

Increasingly, disasters pull rescue workers from around the country to far away sites, and then you are certainly not able to have ready access to your family and friends. But in our modern world of cell phones and computers, it is easier than ever to remain close and feel the support we need.

I stood at the base of the Murrah Federal Building and looked in awe at the destruction. It was several days after the blast and the operation had shifted from rescue to recovery. Still, the rescue workers worked diligently to at least uncover bodies and thereby help families have some answers to their questions. Dust still hung over the site. Generators roared at night to power the bright lights which facilitated a twenty-four-hour, non-stop work commitment. Standing there, I called my friend David, a clinical psychologist. After a week's work with rescue workers and hospital staff, it helped to remain connected to someone as close to me as a brother. It helped to have someone who would listen to me and whose very words of friendship helped me maintain my own personal spiritual and mental health. Daily calls home to my wife also kept me connected to my strongest support system.

Besides receiving support from your loved ones, they are reassured that you are all right. They see the television news reports and have some sense of the risks involved and need to know that you are safe.

7. Give yourself a break. The two weeks I spent at Ground Zero was a gruesome job, but one I believed to be of emotional and spiritual support for families and workers alike. In times of crisis, all of us are able to reach deeply into ourselves and find resources we didn't know we had and work longer and harder than ever before. We find a resilience that transcends our usual capabilities. Even when we are tired and burdened, we discover strength to continue.

But all of us need time to step back and replenish our spirits. It may be making sure that you continue your pattern of running each day, which I did. It may mean spending some time in meditation or watching a show on television that makes you laugh.

At the World Trade Center, each volunteer was able to have one day a week of complete rest. It was remarkably restorative and beneficial. I spent part of my day off at the Metropolitan Museum of Art where I wandered for hours gazing into works of art I had only read about. My work had been in the ruins of tragedy and I had witnessed the consequences of human depravity and the sorrow it causes. When I walked silently through the rooms where some of the most inspiring pieces of art ever created hung, I had a sense that there is hope and beauty. I saw that humans can transcend their sinful nature and bless us with beauty as surely as we are assaulted with sin.

Later in the evening I went to Carnegie Hall where I saw a production of Handel's *Messiah*, and once again experienced the best of human majesty. It is essential to keep perspective and to find a way to refresh yourself.

8. Follow the rules. Clergy who carve out a niche for themselves with cops will always, to some degree, be outsiders no matter how valued and secure is their place on the team. After all, our "home base" is the community of faith, not law enforcement. It is imperative that clergy work collegially within the established protocol.

Clergy are as vulnerable as any other professional when it comes to pushing the boundaries. In Oklahoma City, clergy were to be on scene for a maximum of four hours. But the adrenalin rush was so seductive and the sense of self importance so intense that some clergy blatantly ignored the rules. They overstayed their allotted time. It was bad stewardship of their own resources and it disregarded the clearly stated time frames for clergy to follow.

To counter this, clergy were given hard-hats to wear with color-coded tape indicating which shift they were working and those who overstayed their limits were readily identified and dismissed from service.

Knowing where to go and what sites are out of bounds is essential. We may have created a place in our home or community of such value that there is an open door policy with the officers. But it is important to remember that the rules are likely different when working a major disaster far from home with personnel who do not know you at all.

9. Wear appropriate clothing. This lesson seems absurdly self-explanatory but I include it because it often goes unheeded. Every disaster is different, so no single rule about "appropriate clothing" covers all circumstances.

Disasters are messy. For this reason alone, it will likely mean that the "dress code" includes sturdy shoes, pants and shirts that can withstand the elements and the event itself. Gloves may be quite useful. The chaplain is very unlikely him- or herself to do the work of search and rescue, but it may be likely that the clergy is nevertheless on site and near enough to the disaster that what would be "normal" clothing for one's typical professional work is out of place.

At the DeBruce Grain elevator explosion in Wichita, Kansas, a number of mental health workers volunteered to serve as counselors to the firefighters who were pulling victims out of the explosion or from under tons of grain. Used to working in an office setting where patients keep appointments, a few came to the disaster in business dress including high heels. It was virtually impossible for them to comfortably approach the respite areas where firefighters took breaks because to do so meant long walks over railroad tracks, around heavy equipment, in stifling Kansas summer weather. The next day they were better prepared and dressed appropriately for the setting.

It is generally helpful for chaplains working disasters to have clothing that designates who they are. Clerical collars work for those whose traditions use them. Jackets that say "CHAPLAIN" on them are also useful. At some sites, hard hats that indicate "CHAPLAIN" are worn.

10. Stay centered. Staying connected with your own faith and values is crucial. Disasters are intimidating, unsettling, and can cause people to lose focus. Suffering is no longer an intellectual concept, it is as real as the debris that you ride past on the way to do a blessing for a recovered body. Terrorism is not a news story from a Third World country, it is an event in your own country where you breathe in the dust that hovers over the tragedy. Such things are unsettling to one's faith.

Disaster work calls for one to clarify and define what one truly believes. Maybe for the first time, the bedrock themes of faith are written large and the issues to which we once gave lip service now must be honestly held or tossed aside.

It seems essential to keep in mind that your beliefs work for you, but in disaster work, you will likely work with people (victims as well as helpers) whose faith and values differ from yours. It is important to respect their faith and practice even as you maintain your own.

11. Maintain perspective. When one works a major disaster, it is easy to develop tunnel vision. All one sees is suffering and mayhem. More than one cop has developed a cynical attitude since all he or she deals with, it seems, are people who commit crimes. They also see people who have enough money or influence to navigate their way through and around the court system and avoid the consequences of their actions.

It is important to keep in mind that not everyone is evil. When terrible things are happening, it seems easy to live by stereotypes. In World War II, Japanese Americans were rounded up and imprisoned out of fear that, because they were Japanese, they were automatically suspect. Looking back we realize that that was a horrible mistake, and a comparable contemporary value is to remember that not every Muslim is a terrorist bent on the destruction of America.

12. Respect safety rules. In many disasters, especially ones with large scale destruction, there are built-in risks to watch out for. The air at Ground Zero was filled with toxic substances making it mandatory to wear a mask to filter out tiny particles which could cause injury. Hard hats were also mandatory. Tornados easily rip down power lines leaving "hot" live wires exposed, placing careless workers at risk for electrocution. Gas lines can be severed where they connect with homes increasing the risk of explosions coming from workers who smoke. Exposure to falls causing unexpected cuts or broken bones is also a possibility. Common sense and caution, plus following the rules and regulations, are usually enough to avoid problems.

This is especially important for clergy and mental health professionals who may not be used to crisis work. Law enforcement personnel and paramedics understand the need to follow safety rules; other helpers such as clergy may not even be aware a given rule exists because they lack the knowledge and experience of what the risk factors are.

Some risks are obvious. Only firefighters truly understand how to fight a fire or how to navigate rescues of trapped victims from high-rise buildings. And only law enforcement officers have the equipment and training to handle violent offenders. It is the other, less obvious issues that are easy to overlook.

At the Murrah Building, a retired surgeon who volunteered his time and medical expertise spent a long time with me one evening as we watched the fallen debris being removed from the pile covering the daycare center. After telling me his life story about how he learned to be a strong-willed, "tough" man, athlete, marine, husband, father, and physician, he acknowledged that his toughness left him woefully unprepared to hear or work or relate to others with compassion.

He said to me, "One more thing. Take care of yourself. There are terrible things here that will hurt you. Use a mask to keep out contaminates and be careful where you walk and what you touch. This isn't familiar ground for you and the risks are great."

It was an act of kindness I will never forget. The privilege of working a great tragedy is intoxicating. We go where very few are able to go and we see what most never see. It is essential that we go cautiously. What we offer is worthy, but if we are injured, we can't help.

13. Respect crime scene concerns. Sometimes there are legitimate but competing claims on how best to provide care at a disaster scene. Auto accidents, for example, are occasions when paramedics necessarily contaminate or otherwise compromise evidence on the scene because the extrication of victims is deemed to be a higher priority than worrying too much about trampling skid marks on the gravel road. There are times when legitimate needs compete.

Chaplains are not expected to be experts in investigations or the management of crime scenes. Even clergy with long years' experience in law enforcement and who have established a solid place with a police department are wise to be cautious.

I walked along a row of buildings on a side street near the ruins of the Murrah Federal Building. Most of the windows in the building were shattered. Files were blown open and papers were strewn haphazardly all about the street. The sidewalks were covered with soggy papers, papers which probably came from the insurance company behind the shattered windows. Over the sad city a raw spring storm was building. Low hanging clouds tumbled over one another and the crackle of lightning and the rumble of thunder promised more rain. The developing storm was hurried along with a cold north wind. Rain grew heavier by the minute.

Nearby a group of helpers began to pick up the scattered papers and put them back inside the broken windows of the adjacent office building. They meant well but failed to understand that they were trampling on evidence at a crime scene. Thinking they were helping, they were oblivious to the possibility of disturbing something that might conceivably be of significance.

Presently a few law enforcement personnel on patrol stopped them, checked their credentials and sternly lectured them to *not touch anything*, and to *not enter* any of the offices through the broken windows because, in fact, they were inside a crime scene. While their reason to be there was legitimate, they had strayed from their designated purpose and tried to be helpful, but did so without understanding the significance of their behavior.

14. Stay focused on the supportive care you are allowed to do. Ministry includes a wide range of professional concerns. However, unless otherwise sanctioned, the chaplain's job at a tragedy has a pastoral focus. It is not a time for preaching or for evangelism or any other task, which, while legitimate in ministry in general, is inappropriate in this context.

The chaplain is well served to offer his or her pastoral care through a critical incident stress management (CISM) plan. This is an especially useful intervention modality and works harmoniously with pastoral care.

There are some clergy and lay persons who see disaster work as opportunities to convert people to their faith belief. They have an inadequate understanding of what is needed in disasters from an emotional or spiritual sense, and fail to properly assess and value what is helpful. Some fail to see and understand the ecumenical nature of this work and how a too narrow focus misses the mark.

15. Get adequate rest. Crisis work is exhausting, physically and emotionally. Chaplains doing disaster ministry work are at the front lines of emotional and spiritual trauma. A common misunderstanding is that since the chaplain him- or herself was not a primary victim, then they are basically unscathed. This mindset fails to understand the impact that hearing a steady stream of anguish and sorrow has on those who listen to the stories of survivors. It is a too little understood consequence of crisis care.

At the very least, a chaplain needs to know his or her own limits, and set aside time to rest.

16. Be aware that working a major disaster may call to mind other, previous events from either your personal or professional life and these may be as unsettling to you as is this current tragedy. A couple of days after the Murrah Federal Building explosion my colleague and I did a short defusing with a group of nurses at a local hospital. They had received some of the first victims a couple of days earlier and their nurse manager asked for this session as a way of providing support for them. When the session was over, most of the nurses went on their way. A few lingered to make a comment or to ask a question. I noticed right away one individual who stayed off to himself, watching the other nurses and waiting for the room to clear when he could make a connection with me when the others left.

"Hey Chaplain," he said, trying to be casual and friendly at the same time. "You got a second?" His face told another story. I thought he looked as if he might break into tears.

"Of course," I said.

"Can we find a place to talk?" he asked. We found a quiet room nearby and sat down. With no prompting but rather a sense of dammed up urgency he began.

"I was in Viet Nam. I was a medic there and it was hell. I thought I did pretty well, but what I didn't see was that I began to drink heavily to cope. I made it through Nam, but couldn't stop the drinking when I got home. I had all these demons from Nam haunting me, and I didn't know how to control them. So I drank to shut them out and numb the pain. Finally my wife and the kids ... they left me.

"I got myself into treatment and it helped. My family came back and it all seemed fine, but now this!" With that, he paused and looked away into space. Then he softly said, "With this bombing I'm right back in Nam again. I see the faces all over again. I hear the screaming. I feel like drinking!"

Though he wasn't a primary victim himself, he became an authentic, secondary victim because he re-experienced his own past life and some of the horror wrapped up in his own war days. With encouragement he promised to continue talking about his feelings, get further help, and make use of his AA group and his sponsor.

17. Monitor and manage the intense feelings you may experience. Disasters are sudden, unexpected tragedies that bring death and destruction to whole communities. There are many who assume that because cops and paramedics are professionally trained to work in disasters they are immune to intense feelings. Everyone who works years in disaster care is vulnerable. This does not imply that they are somehow unworthy to do this kind of work. In fact, it only acknowledges their humanity.

A particularly difficult feeling to manage is the excitement one may feel at crisis work. Most other crisis workers will understand. Many others will not. Of course the event is evil. Certainly it is sad. The consequences are widespread and devastating. Without question the work can be gruesome. There is a great satisfaction that comes from knowing you can be of help and hope and comfort in the midst of a catastrophe. Rather than turning away in horror, many of us run toward the event believing we can help.

18. Maintain a sense of humor. This must always be done with great care lest one be misunderstood as being insensitive. The public will not easily understand humor at such a time. They expect compassion, not laughter to prevail.

But trauma surgeons and nurses understand. They often use humor to break the tension and to keep perspective. It is not a matter of ridicule or laughing at victims at all. It is finding a way to lighten the load so that one will not be crippled with the burden of helping others in difficult times.

XI

HEALTH CARE, HOSPITALS, AND CHAPLAINCY

For thirty years my primary professional work was devoted to hospital chaplaincy. During that time I maintained an avid interest in law enforcement chaplaincy and became a reserve officer as well as a chaplain. Such work was not for everyone, but it suited me just fine. Because I worked in the two worlds of health care and law enforcement, I experienced how regularly and essentially they fit together. I believe it is imperative that chaplains who seek to work in these fields appreciate the language and the culture of both. Often law enforcement matters interface with health care issues and the more one understands each world, the more effective the pastoral care will be.

When a patient with multiple gunshot wounds lays on a gurney in the trauma bay, the team of medical experts gathered at his side each attends to some body part or body function. To them, he is the victim of a drive-by shooting. Standing in the doorway to the trauma bay, however, may be police officers—a duty cop, two gang task force members, and a detective. To them, he may be a fugitive wanted for a variety of reasons.

Both the health care professionals and the law enforcement officials have legitimate claims on this person. Sometimes the competing claims need to be smoothed out by someone each side can trust. Frequently a skilled chaplain has credibility with both camps and can help them resolve their issues.

Chaplains who learn how to think systemically, how to avoid being caught in the disagreements and conflicts of others, and how to maintain a non-anxious presence in the context of high anxiety can work wonders in facilitating cooperation between the competing professional groups. It takes effort to build relationships beforehand so that in a crisis, everyone's needs can be addressed when the time is right.

The stories that follow illustrate the inevitable overlap of health care and law enforcement concerns and the place of the chaplain in both.

THE CHAPLAIN IS A BRIDGE

"Level 1 trauma. GSW to chest. Patient is a twenty-year-old male. ETA 1410." Four short phrases told the story of the trauma alert and set in motion an entire trauma team of surgeons, nurses, respiratory therapists, pharmacists, X-Ray technicians, representatives from the blood bank, admissions personnel, and chaplains. More would gather before the event was finished, including the paramedic crew who was bringing in the patient and law enforcement who was working the crime.

This tragedy had occurred in another part of the city. A woman heard shots fired and looked out from her living room window to see a man laying in the yard. Several men were seen speeding away in a dark colored sedan. She called 911 with whatever sketchy details she could give, and that call set in motion the police department and EMS. While that on-scene work was being done, the staff at the hospital where I work scurried to the emergency department and waited in Trauma Room 1.

I stood in the hall peering through the frosted glass doors in front of the trauma rooms, in the emergency department, waiting for the patient's arrival. It didn't take long. A paramedic walked briskly at either end of the gurney, guiding it from the ambulance through the doors and into the hallway. A third paramedic administered chest compressions as they walked. A fourth worked the bag mask resuscitator squeezing oxygen into the critically injured man. Their serious faces acknowledged the severity of the event. It was a "grab and go" call.

Blood seeped through his shirt and large splotches covered the gurney. Some dripped onto the floor as they rushed him head first into the trauma bay. Quickly and deftly he was moved from the ambulance gurney to the trauma table, where the team began their work. I stood at the back of the room near the recording nurse. The chaplain's role must be offered in concert with the medical staff whose job is to seek to save the life of a desperately wounded stranger. My job would begin later.

A respiratory therapist inserted an intubation tube. A nurse took over CPR. Vital signs were taken from the electronic notices that came from the equipment attached to the unmoving patient. X Rays were ordered to determine the severity of the gunshot wounds.

"I count seven entry wounds," acknowledged the trauma surgeon to the recording nurse, "but only four exit wounds."

The paramedic who had accompanied the patient in the ambulance stood by me. "See that?" she said as she pointed to the urine bag. She was talking to a pharmacy student who was watching his first level 1 GSW and who seemed both excited and apprehensive. "It's bright red," she said.

"And that's not good?" he asked.

"No. Something's been nicked and he's bleeding out inside."

"Belly's distended and hard," said the surgeon. "We need to get to surgery right away."

Another trauma surgeon slipped the fresh chest X Rays onto the screen and the two surgeons and their residents clustered around the black and white pictures to learn their secrets. Two bullets could be seen resting ominously near the heart. The primary surgeon spoke to the rest. "The bullets may have clipped the heart. That's probably where the blood's coming from. But he's got a belly wound, too, so maybe it's his intestine."

I continued to stand back. Soon I would have to contact family members and summon them to the hospital. There they would wait anxious hours of uncertainty, not knowing if they would be blessed with a recovery, or if they would face life without a loved one. And sometimes they must contend with a loved one whose life has been unalterably changed for the worse with paralysis or some other radical incapacitation. Maybe they would have to live with the bitter reality that their loved one was somehow involved with misconduct that resulted in his death or injury. Or maybe he or she was an innocent victim who would forever pay a price for someone else's mean spirit.

Whatever the cause, the consequences can be devastating for survivors. And that's where my job begins. Until then, I try to offer support to the staff, and that includes the police officers who were on scene and who have the difficult and risky job of securing it and making it safe for the arriving paramedics and the EMS crew. Without the help of these paramedics and EMS, and their preliminary diagnosis, nothing of consequence would happen later. The golden hour of possibility starts in the field with those in the front line of emergency care.

PARAMEDICS—A TRIBUTE

Too few people understand the reality of the paramedic's job. The work of critical care often begins in a driving snow storm with a bone-chilling north wind and temperatures so cold that your fingers feel like sticks. The road can be so slick and icy that passers-by slide perilously close to paramedics as they work furiously to open a car and extricate a wounded victim. Their lives are also at risk from the curious public who drive by gawking at the scene and driving inattentively.

It is often dirty where paramedics work to save lives. Hospital staff may say later, "That's an odd smell. Wonder what it is? Smells like diesel fuel." Sometimes it's difficult for other medical professionals to grasp the reality of front-line, on-the-scene crisis care, which is a world apart from the hospital. Hospital staffs provide first rate care to the wounded, but they do so in safe surroundings with a highly trained medical team and a host of technology. The sterile cleanliness of a surgical suite is wishful thinking in the field where fuel and grain and road dust and stones mix with open wounds. The work of the paramedic sometimes comes only after the fire is out, but the wreckage still smolders. The victims must still be recovered from the twisted metal now perilously resting on blocks and jacks.

And with a shooting, like there was today, the potential danger of still more shooting must be considered. Gang violence has no respect for decency, or the lives of innocents. Until they need help, most people don't understand the rigor of the paramedic's work.

When today's patient was removed to surgery, I asked the paramedic standing nearby what it was like at the scene. She thought for a moment, then said, "It was tough. We're used to arriving and providing care immediately. But some scenes are like this one and we had to 'stand off' until the police checked the area. There's always the potential for one of us to get hurt so we understand. But still, we have to wait until it's safe and the waiting puts the patient at risk." Then she continued, "And the cops all have guns and vests for protection. We don't. You feel vulnerable out there and we have to depend on them for safety. And we understand and accept that. But every minute counts."

In a little while, the housekeeping staff came and cleaned up the trauma room. The police removed the clothing for evidence. The equipment was taken to be sterilized. The bloody litter was removed for a wash down. The white board was erased so that the next trauma's information could be written on it. I escorted the police officer to surgery where he expected to collect the bullets for evidence upon their extraction, then walked back to my office and wondered when the name of the unidentified patient would be known so I could get on with the rest of my work. And the paramedics? Still on duty ... awaiting their next call.

A DRUG DEAL GONE BAD

The shrill tones of the trauma pager awakened me in the middle of the night as I slept in the on-call room at Wesley. I sat at the edge of the bed clearing my head and looked at the message screen on the pager.

"Level 1 trauma. GSW to chest and legs. ETA 15 min." Time enough to dress and speculate on what was coming in. Someone had been shot in the chest and legs, was in critical condition, and would arrive within minutes. I took my position at the back of the trauma room and watched the nurse write on the board the additional information the medical team needed to know, which was radioed in by the paramedic on scene. It, too, was cryptic but ominous:

Multiple GSWs to chest and legs

CPR IN PROGRESS

Code blue on scene

BP 80/30

The notes contained only medical information, but verbally the nurse added, "PD suspects it was a drug deal that went bad. Patient is a known user and dealer."

The trauma room rapidly filled with the surgery residents, the house physicians, numerous nurses, radiology technicians, respiratory therapists, and security. I moved outside to wait for the ambulance to arrive.

Hospital security was already standing watch on the drive and just inside the hall between the outside door and the trauma room. It is a sign of the times that when violent acts occur, our security officers take a heightened approach to the incident. No one says anything, but it feels safer to believe that while you focus single-mindedly on the victim, someone else is watching your back. Sometimes all this security seems melodramatic, but most agree that it is good to be prudent.

The sliding glass doors of our emergency department were frosted, making it impossible to see in or out. Years ago they were clear glass, making it easy to see into the trauma room; but with the rise of violence, they were changed so visibility was obscured. It was hoped that being out of sight might lessen the risk of violence coming into the trauma room. Just outside, the ambulance turned in the drive and stopped outside the doors. Its red lights still flashed. The victim was wheeled through the double doors, down the hallway, and into Wesley Trauma Room 1. I stood aside as they passed.

One paramedic continued chest compressions as he walked. Another held a plastic container of medicine high overhead so it would flow into the patient's veins in a valiant attempt to sustain his life. A firefighter walked on either end and guided the gurney, leaving a trail of blood from the ambulance, down the hall, and into the trauma room. Physicians began to give orders and a nurse furiously wrote everything down to keep the information accurate.

Everyone in the trauma room has a job to do, and I watch to understand which staff members might benefit from follow-up later on.

More than most, this scene was a bloody mess. Pools of blood gathered on the floor, and the trauma team had no choice but to walk through them, leaving bloody footprints throughout the room. The paramedics were covered in blood—they had been exposed at the scene itself, and then gave CPR in the ambulance all the way to the hospital. A nurse quickly cut the victim's clothes off. His left leg seemed barely attached. If I hadn't known better, I might have thought the patient had been attacked by a large animal. His chest was peppered with holes—someone had apparently shot him point blank. I wondered what this split second event must have been like and what prompts people to try to resolve their problems with such violence.

Trauma rooms are incredible places. At first glance it seems that the entire scene is chaotic. Medical staff focus on body parts. A respiratory therapist checks the victim's breathing. A surgeon orders X Rays and then technicians place X Ray plates underneath the victim's chest. Another physician uses Doppler equipment to listen for a pulse in the nearly severed left leg and, hearing none, says to the gathered medical team, "No pulse in the left leg. We gotta get him to surgery ASAP! Finish up quickly!"

Another surgeon makes an assessment about the man's chest and determines that his lungs are filling with fluid and he needs a chest tube immediately or he won't survive to make it to surgery. A nurse hands her a sterile container with a scalpel which she removes. She then quickly sprays an antiseptic on the patient's chest and with one quick, hard, but deft slice, she opens the right thoracic area exposing the raw secrets of his chest cavity and lungs. Other young residents gather around to watch this procedure. Someday it will be their job to do the cutting.

"X Ray!" yells the technician. Usually that is a signal for me and others to step aside. A few do move to shield themselves from the invisible rays which both help save lives but, over time, accumulate and cause potential problems for the helpers. In the rush to save a life, some personal precautions are overlooked. People stay focused on their task and often disregard the unseen danger to themselves.

I notice that the city police have arrived. Some are in brown uniforms. One is in a dark blue jump suit; he carries a camera. Still another is in bluejeans with a silver star on his left side and a Glock model 26 on the other side. He wears a bright yellow t-shirt with block letters on the back indicating that he is with the sheriff's department. All those involved in this trauma are part of my pastoral responsibilities.

One of the officers confirms the preliminary report. "Looks like it was a drug deal gone bad. He got set up. We've got a description of the car and a license number so that should help."

"Let's roll," yells the chief resident. I move back and a host of physicians and nurses rush by to an awaiting elevator where they accompany the patient to surgery. Two housekeeping personnel wait quietly with mops and buckets to clean up the carnage. They are the silent helpers who are never acknowledged.

"Glad this one's over," said one nurse.

The officer with the camera said, "Any chance I can get a picture of him before they operate?"

"Check with the OR nurse. Maybe they'll let you in before they start." Then turning to me, "Tom, can you take him there?"

The officer's work was just starting. There were pictures to take, an investigation to piece together, evidence to gather, and interviews with witnesses to set up. If all went well, there would be arrests and a trial.

And the paramedic? The one covered with blood who did chest compressions? He noticed, after it was all over, that he had received a cut on a finger sometime in the process, and was consequently exposed to a potential blood-borne disease. He must wait to see if the victim was HIV positive or had some other disease and then be screened until he passed the current standard for a safe and secure waiting period. Until then, each day would be filled with anxiety. Cops, firefighters, and paramedics all take risks to serve the public.

As for the victim, his troubles were clearly just beginning, assuming he survived this devastating ordeal at all. He would likely lose his leg and need to learn to meet life in a whole new way. He would probably spend time in jail, and I wondered if he would think all this was worth it.

Although he came into our hospital as "Unknown Ed," he wouldn't remain so for very long. Soon enough we would know his identity. Someone would have to notify his family that he was here. Unless they found out through the web of connections that exist on the street or from the police chaplain, it would likely be my task to notify his family. And they would come and stand at his bedside and watch helplessly as their son or husband lingered between vitality and helplessness.

And likely as not, my trauma pager would sound again, and another trauma would unfold before my eyes. Once more the hospital staff and the cops and I would meet. I saw no end to this sorrow.

LEE'S STORY

I stood beside the crib and watched the tiny child. Wires were taped to his chest to monitor his heart rate. His fluid intake and output were carefully noted. A respirator controlled his breathing and kept him alive. Neonatal intensive care nurses kept a close watch on this child, as they did every infant in their care whose start in life has been radically altered. In this case, the placenta connecting the baby to his mother prematurely separated, resulting in a lack of oxygen to his brain of undetermined duration. He was born by emergency Caesarian section a Code Blue.

It was November 27, 1995, and for the past twenty years I had been present at an unknown number of local and national disasters dealing with trauma and heartbreak. I had done my best in all those experiences to provide competent and professional care, mostly to people I had never met, but who were in the midst of a life-altering crisis. But as I stood at the crib of this tiny child, Elias Anthony Estrada, I was filled with grief and anger, fear and helplessness. This was no stranger. He was our first grandson. What had been a normal pregnancy just hours before, turned suddenly into a high risk birth.

I knew from my work in the PICU that other children who were casualties of abruptions often had devastating consequences. Depending on the length of the oxygen deprivation, they could have brain damage causing a lifetime of delayed development, blindness, or hearing loss. The gift of a healthy child could turn in a moment to a lifetime of altered expectations.

Earlier that morning I had received a call from Terrie, the baby's paternal grandmother, telling me that our daughter Sara was experiencing problems, and was taken to the hospital. I felt comfort hearing the calm way she told me, but beneath her reassuring voice was the crystal clear message that this was an impending tragedy and we must be there. I was at work thirty miles away, and Linda, my wife, had the day off and was also in Wichita, buying Christmas presents. I called security at the mall and they were able to page her. We sped north in two cars.

It's amazing how we may react in times of crisis. Contrary to my theology in normal times, I had the ridiculous feeling that this was unfair. Because I had devoted a lifetime of caring for very ill children I wanted a favor from God for the work I had done. I promised years more of dedication if just this one child might survive. And Linda was saying her own prayers, making her own bargains and promises, and wishing she could use her knowledge as a physical therapist to do everything she could to help the baby. And none of it was in our control.

I had taken a nonchalant attitude about becoming a grandparent. I was neither excited nor disinterested, but kept my distance from the event and, frankly, couldn't see any reason for it to have much bearing on my life. Maybe that disassociation had something to do with the fact that my father had died a few years before, and my mother was not going to survive for many more months. (Four as it turned out.)

But on this November day as I stood at the bassinet of this tiny child, out of the depths of my soul I felt an overwhelming anguish. My spirit seemed broken and I worried for my daughter, the baby's father, my wife, but mostly for the infant whose future was unknown.

I wanted every normal thing for my grandson. I wanted him to roll over and one day walk. I wanted him to learn to say my name. I wanted to watch him ride a bike and play ball. I wanted to hear about his day at school. I wanted every ordinary event that other children had. But I knew at that moment that whatever happened, whatever level of function he was able to achieve, I would love him with all my heart.

Suddenly the idea came to me that I wanted to baptize my grandson. I knew that he was born in innocence and love and was pure in heart and soul, but I wanted him to receive God's blessing anyway. So when the nurses were busy with another child, I touched my finger to my eyes and baptized my grandson with my tears.

That was years ago. And for whatever reason, maybe as a gift from God, maybe due to his excellent medical care, probably not because I'd tried to be a good person, Lee learned to roll over. He learned to play ball. He does well in school. He teases his brothers and his sister. He's a teenager now. He has a kind heart and a sweet, sensitive spirit.

And I think of him whenever I see a sick or injured child and know how fortunate we are.

UNKNOWN VICKY

I read the cryptic message as it scrolled across my pager: "Level 1 trauma. Twenty-five- to thirty-year-old female. GSW to head. ETA 7 minutes."

Seven minutes to get ready. It's not that I have much to get ready for, but I value the time to emotionally prepare myself. It helps to have the right attitude in place. Traumas are horrible events that unfold in seconds and leave a lifetime of consequences that change the destinies of people. Some of these people are the victims of the tragedies. Some will be family members. Some are hospital workers. Some will be in law enforcement. All of us will be touched. I try to remain aware of this.

The unspoken horror of everyone who works in a hospital or in law enforcement is that the patient being brought in is a friend or relative rather than a stranger. I steel myself for that possibility. After all, I have a thirty-year-old daughter. What if, God forbid, it is her? I hurried to the emergency department.

A multitude of people quickly gathered—physicians, surgeons, pharmacy, a respiratory therapist, two SICU nurses, a few medical students. Some came running, some walking briskly.

And then the patient arrived. Two paramedics wheeled this bleeding and lifeless person in, while a third did chest compressions and a fourth squeezed the bag mask, hoping against the odds to keep her alive.

As I stepped aside, I closed the curtain to keep curious eyes from unnecessary gawking. Even the deeply wounded in a trauma room deserve privacy, although that comes in small measures. In a trauma, you are stripped of your clothing, your dignity, your health, and well being. Sometimes you can't even breathe for yourself.

"One, two, three, lift" ordered one paramedic, and with that the patient was moved from the EMS gurney to the trauma bed. As the staff began the necessary medical intervention, her clothes were cut off and she was covered with warm blankets.

"She was Code Blue when we arrived and we've done CPR ever since," reported a paramedic to the surgeon.

"She was just leaving a convenience store when someone screamed at her, took out a hand gun, and shot her. Then he took off in his car. She's been hit once in the head and twice in the chest. A customer saw the whole thing and called it in. She doesn't have an ID, and so far we don't know who she is. She doesn't have a purse, so it may have been a robbery, but we don't know."

Turning to the officer who arrived when the ambulance did, the surgeon asked, "Do we know what kind of gun it was?"

"Yes," responded the officer. "Casings on the asphalt were .357 shells. Pretty good size. Especially to the head."

No one said anything, but we all worried. "I need a Stat X Ray!" ordered the physician. "There's a significant wound to the head and only one exit wound from the chest. I need another warm blanket and I need an operating room, Stat! We need to know where the bullet is. And I need a neurosurgeon," she continued.

"Do we have an airway?" the surgeon asked.

"Working on it!" yelled a respiratory therapist. Sweat soaked his blue shirt as he worked feverishly to insert the breathing tube in her throat. "Got it!" he said.

Soon enough a host of law enforcement officials arrived: two duty officers who had responded to the scene, a detective in a trench coat talking on his cell phone, and an investigator in a black uniform who said to a nurse, "Can I get pictures? I won't be in the way. I need permission, though." I liked his willingness to try to find a collegial way to do his job with an understanding that right now her treatment was more important than his pictures.

Carefully, the investigator slipped between two nurses and snapped a picture. Moving aside, he took another view. Then another.

"We gotta roll!" ordered the surgeon. "She needs surgery *now*! This one's touch and go as it is," she remarked.

"Any family?" asked another physician to me. "Not yet," I replied. "She's still unknown," I added.

I hate it that somewhere there are people who love her and who would want to be here with her. But sometimes it happens that people remain in the company of strangers even in their darkest hour.

"Doctor?" said the detective. "We really need the bullets if you get them. They're evidence. If you could save them and her clothes, too, we sure need them."

It all makes a difference—the emergency care of the patient, the collection of evidence, the family notification. Each piece has its place in the process. But right now, the most urgent need was surgery. "Unknown Vicky," the hospital name assigned to this stranger until her real identity was discovered, was quickly and steadily drifting farther away from life and plummeting into the world beyond. Time and a medical miracle seemed to be her only hope, and both were sadly remote. Maybe prayer was the only answer.

Police work is never just with criminals any more than medical work is just with patients. Ultimately, both professions involve husbands, wives, parents, children, friends, and other loved ones. There is always a technical dimension to any professional job. But the human element is the bedrock of everything. That's especially true for chaplains.

We contemporary humans want storybook endings that are happy. These make us feel good because all our hard work has paid off and we feel confident and satisfied. But there are occasions when the best we do is not enough. As I waited with the investigating officer just outside the surgery suite, we chatted about the scratch on his hand that he got breaking up a fight at the detention center the night before. It was idle talk to pass the time.

"Chaplain," said the nurse at the desk. "It's surgery. She didn't make it. They just pronounced her."

So it was over. Unknown Vicky was dead. The investigation would continue, but now it was for a murder and not just a shooting. We would continue to look for family, but the hope to save her life was gone. Unknown Vicky had died an unnecessary and violent death. And a multitude of strangers did their best to help, but this time it wasn't enough.

A SHAKEN BABY SYNDROME

I arrived early and took a seat in the seminar room. Shortly, the other childcare team members arrived and we chatted amicably, waiting for the meeting to begin. This social small talk served the purpose of managing the feelings that all of us carried into the room. Soon enough we would share our knowledge of the abuse that a tiny one-year-old had experienced, and the resulting severe limitation he would live with forever. Our primary purpose would be to review the incident, explore the medical consequences, look at the social implications for the child, and hear about the legal ramifications.

There would be little joy in this meeting, and we all tried to set aside our sadness and outrage. How could such a thing happen? We needed to think clearly about how to help this gravely impaired child lying five floors above us in the pediatric intensive care unit, and hanging onto his new life by a thread.

Dr. Murdock asked us to begin our meeting with introductions. The childcare team includes representatives from law enforcement, the Social and Rehabilitative Services of the state of Kansas, the county attorney's office, and the hospital staff. Every discipline and every profession has an important perspective and responsibility.

Dr. Murdock began with a review of the basic facts as best they were known. A young family received a call from their child's babysitter telling them that she had called 911 because the child appeared to have had a seizure and had stopped breathing. After a brief stay in an outlying hospital's emergency department, the infant was flown to our facility for more intensive care.

At first everyone who had anything to do with the child was of interest to the police. After all, a significant assault was determined to have occurred and no one was accepting responsibility. Everyone was quick to blame someone else. The only known truth was that a one-year-old child lingered with brain damage and an almost certain blindness, losses which would last a lifetime.

The radiologist had the worst news of all. The injuries were a textbook example of a "shaken baby syndrome," including the massive retinal hemorrhages which would likely leave the child blind. There were other injuries which might result in brain damage, though the severity of that was yet to be determined. Older injuries were noted, suggesting that the child had likely been previously abused.

The radiologist concluded her findings and sat down. For a

while we looked at the CT scans, still on the viewing screen, in stunned silence. The medical staff in attendance knew full well the technical implications of the injuries and the lingering, limiting consequences. The rest of us didn't have to have a medical degree to comprehend. An uncontrolled adult had shaken this tiny child until all hopes for a healthy and normal life were destroyed.

I have heard this story too many times. I have watched too many small children try to find their way back from the terror of abuse ... frequently at the hands of an adult who ought to have loved them. And then their lives are temporarily in the hands of strangers who try their best to reclaim for them as much hope and possibility as they can.

***

The job of law enforcement in these tragedies is often a quiet, under-appreciated job because it involves sensitive and skilled interviewing to adequately uncover the truth. It is a job done when feelings are raw and blame is high. It is a job done when people are extremely defensive. Even if one isn't guilty of the violation itself, many wonder and worry if they could have prevented the tragedy if only they had made other choices. And it is a job that is done most of the time with a personal awareness of one's own anger. How in God's name can an adult shake a baby so hard that the still forming brain liquefies, and the tiny eyes detach or hemorrhage?

Law enforcement represents that part of our culture which says that, as best we can, we will look out for the blind, the lame, the halt, the infants, the frail elderly, the injured; and that when anyone offends such vulnerable ones, society will seek some redress on their behalf. That someone is the law enforcement community. It is law enforcement which is assigned the responsibility to see to it that care for the least, the lost, and the lonely is not overlooked or abused. Though the actual care occurs elsewhere, law enforcement is the guardian of the process. This responsibility is shared with families and the faith communities, and that is why chaplains are a part of this secular community which nevertheless works at a sacred task.

But it is difficult work. Often as not the alleged perpetrator is less evil than inept, less mean-spirited than overwhelmed. In such moments there are two victims: the abused child who will pay for the rest of his life, and the offending adult who lost his or her way in a moment of weakness, and will live with the guilt of this behavior. Such a shame smolders forever. Upon occasion the perpetrator actually is a mean-spirited person who cares nothing for the victim. Then the consequences of justice seem most appropriate.

After an hour the meeting ended. The medical staff went back to the unit to continue offering medical interventions in hopes that, with enough effort, at least there would be no more loss of vitality. The SRS (Social and Rehabilitation Services) went about their task of notifying other families in the childcare network about what had happened. The two detectives prepared to conduct more interviews, seeking to capture the truth which for the moment was hidden underneath guilt so overwhelming and shame so oppressive that it was hard to find.

And I would go upstairs to console the heartbroken parents. They were thought to be innocent, but were left devastated as they learned that their babysitter, whom they trusted, could have done such a thing. They would have to find a whole new way to raise their child in light of this unspeakable tragedy, and all the broken dreams that just now made life seem unbearable.

ACKNOWLEDGEMENTS

Thirty years of crisis care with cops is a long time to devote to the task of bringing hope and healing to deeply troubled people. Such a task inevitably took me into the depths of great sorrow and anguish in the homes of strangers. I remain profoundly touched by all those who allowed me to enter their lives in times of their vulnerability, raw feelings, and deep emotions. It is their stories I have told and I thank them.

Almost every Saturday evening during those thirty years I spent with one local law enforcement agency or another for both routine ride-alongs and emergency calls. I was accepted and included like a brother. They became many of my closest friends and I remain a strong supporter of all my law enforcement colleagues. They received me, confided in me, watched over me, laughed with me, gave me care when my own life was troubled. And I thank them all for allowing me to work beside them and become a part of them.

I offer a special thanks to my work colleagues at Prairie View Mental Health Center and Wesley Medical Center for giving me time away from work to provide crisis care in other settings. I always knew that I carried their good wishes with me wherever I went.

My family supported this passion of mine, said goodbye on Saturday nights, and were concerned about me while I was gone. I could not have done this work without them. I always carried Kimberly, Mark, Michael, and Sara with me.

I am especially appreciative of the love and support of my wife Linda, who has been my companion and friend for almost five decades. She has encouraged my dreams, supported my work and touched my heart.

Finally, I thank my editor at Hohm Press, Regina Sara Ryan, for her keen eye for detail, her steady support, and her kind heart.

INDEX

A

absence of God. *See* God
assault, 78-80
author's feelings. *See* chaplain, feelings in response to job
automobile accidents, 10, 48-50, 51-56, 115-119, 149-155

B

blessing, 23, 149, 164-166, 196
bombing. *See* Oklahoma City; terrorism
building search, 34-38, 66-73

C

chaplain
  as bridge, 110, 141, 186-88
  as representative of church, 61, 161
  authority of. *See* pastoral authority
  beliefs of, *x-xi*, 180
  in someone else's world, *xi-xiii*, 26-27, 39-41, 55-56, 61, 133, 178-179, 186
  knowing themselves, x-xii, 26-27, 42, 51, 107-108, 176
  feelings in response to job, *xiv*-v, 87-91, 110-112, 118-119, 125- 126, 138-143, 185, 194-197
  and self-care, 174-175, 182-184
  support for, 165, 175-178
  See also hospital chaplaincy
children
  abuse of, 199-201

death of, 5, 11, 101, 107-111, 139-153, 160, 162-163
high-risk birth of, 194-196
as survivors, 99, 105-106, 118, 134-138,
witnessing violence, *ix, xiv-xv*, 14, 19, 21
CISM (Critical Incident Stress Management), 83-86, 161, 167, 173-185
clergy, *ix-x*, 1, 11, 23, 157, 173, 176, 178, 183
  and emergency ministry, 26-38
clinical pastoral care (definition), *x-xi*
community, 2, 58, 82-87, 118, 122, 177, 179, 201
  created in times of crisis, 169, 172, 175-176
  faith __, 22, 51, 62, 94, 155, 157, 161, 178
  law enforcement __, *xi-xiii*, 1, 3, 82, 201-202
compassion, 17, 98
  in death notification, 132, 134, 138-139, 142, 150, 153
  of police, *xv, xvi*, 5, 49, 51, 83, 89, 106, 150
confession, 19
cooperation (among crisis professionals), 58, 72, 125, 176, 186, 188-190, 198- 199
cops. *See* police officers
courage, 26, 55, 59-60, 78, 93, 115
  of chaplain, 2, 57, 78, 91
  of crisis professionals, *xiv*, 59-60, 67, 85, 95
  to grieve, 7-8
credibility (with police), xii, 39, 52, 61, 64, 186. *See also* police, perspective of

204

ABOUT THE AUTHOR

Dr. Thomas Shane is a graduate of Yale and Vanderbilt Divinity School. For thirty years he was a board certified hospital chaplain (APC) and a certified clinical pastoral educator (ACPE). His chaplaincy was divided between a psychiatric hospital and a large medical/trauma center. Dr. Shane also worked as a commissioned law enforcement officer, as a chaplain to several agencies. His work in law enforcement took him into the usually hidden worlds of violence, suffering, moral issues and disaster, and here he brought pastoral comfort where it was most needed but least expected. He is the author of: *When Life Meets Death: Stories of Death and Dying, Truth and Courage.* The father of four grown children, Dr. Shane lives with his wife in Kingwood, Texas.

ABOUT HOHM PRESS

HOHM PRESS is committed to publishing books that provide readers with alternatives to the materialistic values of the current culture, and promote self-awareness, the recognition of interdependence, and compassion. Our subject areas include parenting, religious studies, women's studies, the arts and poetry. Our affiliate **Kalindi Press** presents titles in the fields of natural health and nutrition, gender studies, and the acclaimed *Family and World Health Series*, for children and parents.

Contact Information: Hohm Press, P.O. Box 2501, Prescott, AZ 86302 US • 928-778-9189 • hppublisher@cableone.net www.hohmpress.com and www.kalindipress.com